# A
# PRACTICAL
# CHRISTIANITY

# A

# PRACTICAL

# CHRISTIANITY

*MEDITATIONS FOR*

*THE SEASON OF LENT*

## JANE SHAW

FOREWORD BY
BR. CURTIS ALMQUIST, SSJE

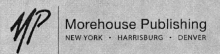
Morehouse Publishing
NEW YORK · HARRISBURG · DENVER

Unless otherwise noted, the Scripture quotations contained herein are from the New Revised Standard Version Bible, copyright © 1989 by the Division of Christian Education of the National Council of Churches of Christ in the U.S.A. Used by permission. All rights reserved.

Morehouse Publishing, 4775 Linglestown Road, Harrisburg, PA 17112
Morehouse Publishing, 445 Fifth Avenue, New York, NY 10016
Morehouse Publishing is an imprint of Church Publishing Incorporated.

www.churchpublishing.org

Cover art: John Olsen, *Lake Hindmarsh, the Wimmera* (1970). Used by permission.

Cover design by Laurie Klein Westhafer
Typeset by Denise Hoff

Library of Congress Cataloging-in-Publication Data

Shaw, Jane, 1963–
A practical Christianity : meditations for the season of Lent / Jane Shaw.
    p. cm.
  Includes bibliographical references.
  ISBN 978-0-8192-2776-8 (pbk.) -- ISBN 978-0-8192-2777-5 (ebook)
1. Lent--Meditations.  I. Title.
  BV85.S465 2012
  242'.34--dc23

                              2011038938

Printed in the United States of America

10  9  8  7  6  5  4  3  2  1

*For Vincent Strudwick*
*dear and constant friend,*
*wise counselor and*
*mentor in all things*

# Contents

# Foreword

Jesus shows remarkably little interest in people's spiritual lives. He is, however, passionate about people's lives—who, what, how they are *in toto*: their body, mind, and soul. Jesus promises to be with us always, wherever and however we are. If we are going to be present to Jesus' real presence—and not just virtually present—we need to find practices for "being there," living life as an ongoing invitation from God. Whether we work, or walk, or weep, or wait, God is with us. Many of us need periodic reminders of this truth. Lent can be a great help to retrieve, recover, redeem what is most important to us, yet may have gotten lost along the way.

The season of Lent begins at the Ash Wednesday liturgy with a prayer derived from Psalm 51: "Create and make in us new and contrite hearts . . ." The English word, "contrite," comes from the Latin, *contritus*, which means "thoroughly crushed." The sense of the word is not about a broken heart, but rather, a heart broken open. It's a double metaphor. This is a bidding to God, asking for God's aid in our own heart's being broken open to the needs of the world that surrounds us, a world that God so loves. It is also a prayer to retrieve, recover, and redeem what is most important—in this case, to be given a like-new heart. This is not a heart bypass procedure. Rather, this is a thoroughfare right through our heart—spiritual angioplasty—with every vessel and valve completely unclogged, pumping afresh with the light and life and love of God.

Jane Shaw's *A Practical Christianity* is a great aid for this Lenten endeavor. We do not need help making life more difficult than it already is. She knows this. Jane is encouraging, faithful, and streetwise, helping us hone a Lenten practice that brings into a graceful harmony our relationship with our own self, with others, and with God, as we anticipate the gift of joy at Eastertide. She has forensic insight about rejection and disappointment, resentment and bitterness; she shares delight with poetry and stories full of wonder; she extols the grace of forgiveness and the redemption of failure; she addresses the problem of certainty and the liberation of paradox; she helps us claim the here-and-now and, at the same time, look to the glory of life to come, "life after dust."

The name of the church season, Lent, does not have a religious etymology. Lent literally means "long days." The word comes from a prehistoric West Germanic root signifying spring, an allusion to the lengthening of days at this time of year in the northern hemisphere. The season of Lent can be very helpful in clearing out debris in our soul's closet as we prepare for Easter. On the other hand, the actual length of Lent—40 days—can become tedious, onerous, fraught with well-intended disciplines gone amuck. Drawing on her own formation and practice, Jane Shaw proves to be a wonderful Lenten companion, a combination of sage, mentor, cheerleader, and spiritual mother.

Br. Curtis Almquist, SSJE
Society of St. John the Evangelist
Cambridge, Massachusetts

# Acknowledgments

This book began as the Brown Lectures at First Presbyterian Church in Dallas, Texas, in 2005. I am grateful to Bill Carl, the Senior Pastor there at the time, for his kind invitation to deliver the lectures, and to all those who gave me much to think about in their responses to my talks. My thanks, too, for the kindness and warm hospitality shown to me by my hosts there, especially Charles and (the late) Peggy Craft.

I revised the lectures and gave them as a Lenten series at Grace Cathedral, San Francisco, in 2011, where I received many helpful comments from members of the congregation there, for which my thanks. The thinking that informed the final version of this book has also been worked out in sermons preached at New College, Oxford, Christ Church Cathedral in Oxford, and Grace Cathedral in San Francisco. Feedback from the congregations in all of those places has been invaluable.

Stephanie Spellers persuaded me to turn the lectures into a short book and she has been a fabulous editor: encouraging in all ways, and offering excellent advice and suggestions at every stage of the writing and editing process. She even took time out of her own vacation to read drafts of chapters. Her thoughtful comments and careful editing made this a much better book than it otherwise might have been. It has been a pleasure to work with her. Sarah Ogilvie was, as always, the finest of critics and conversation partners: she and I have spent many hours discussing the themes of this book. Kathy Anderson, my literary agent in America, has done her usual wonderful job of helping the process of publication go smoothly. Daphne Tooke, my excellent assistant at Grace Cathedral who helps me manage my multi-faceted life as the Dean of a cathedral, an academic, and a writer, helped with permissions. Sara Miles read a preliminary draft of the manuscript and offered helpful and illuminating suggestions, as always. John Olsen kindly took the time to talk to me about painting and his work as an artist when I met with him in 2005, and more recently gave permission for his wonderful painting to be used as the cover of this book. I am very grateful to him and to his son Tim Olsen for making that possible. Deborah Hart, Senior Curator at the National Gallery of Art in Canberra, offered her time and expertise in talking to me about the work of both Grace Cossington Smith and John Olsen, for which I am thankful. And finally, thank you to Ryan Masteller, at Church Publishing, who managed this manuscript through the publication process with great efficiency and grace.

I dedicate this book to Vincent Strudwick, with love and thanks for his friendship over many years.

# Introduction

# A Practical Christianity

For the earliest converts to Christianity, the question before they were baptized and joined the Christian community was not so much "What do you believe?" as "How has your life been transformed?" In some churches in the third century, the lives of catechumens—those being prepared for baptism—were examined with the following questions being put to their sponsor: "Have they lived good lives when they were catechumens? Have they honored the widows? Have they visited the sick? Have they done every kind of good work?"[1]

This period of preparation could last up to three years. Not surprisingly, after such a long build up, baptism was a startling and transformative event. In many places this initiation occurred on Easter Eve. At this Vigil gathering, the newly baptized emerged from the baptismal waters, were marked with the sign of the cross with oil, and in some places were given milk and honey, and even blessed cheese, and they were allowed for the *first* time into the Eucharist.

To put practice before belief is surprising to us. We live

in a post-Protestant age in which "right" belief has taken precedence. Christianity is now often presented as a doctrinal religion, in which you have to believe six impossible things before breakfast to be allowed into the special club known as The Church. We also live in a post-Enlightenment world. The rise of science and the Enlightenment pressed the faithful to ask whether they could logically believe in x or y doctrine (miracles, prophecy, the virgin birth, the Incarnation, the creation account in Genesis) or not. Science and philosophy forced the question of belief. Truth became a matter of logic and rationality rather than the reality of transformation. This insistence on the primacy of belief, coupled with an emphasis on the need to believe certain doctrines, can be very off-putting for those approaching Christianity for the first time, as well as Christians of long standing.

But this is not how it was for the earliest Christians. They were converted to faith because Christianity transformed their lives. Some, for example, found their lives were changed by the kindness of Christian strangers. Consider Pachomius in early fourth-century Egypt. He was in prison after being press-ganged into military service. Local Christians heard the prisoners were in distress and took them food, drink, clothing and other necessities. Pachomius asked what was going on. He was told that the people coming to his aid were Christians, who were merciful to everyone, including strangers. He was so convinced of the truth of Christianity by their actions that once he was discharged from the army, he was baptized and became one of the founding figures of Christian monasticism, building communities up and down the River Nile.[2]

Of course theology emerged from and in the early churches. The church fathers (as they are usually called) such as Irenaeus, Origen, Augustine, and Gregory of Nyssa wrestled with the big questions about the nature of Jesus (Was he human? divine? both?); salvation (What was the relationship between works and grace?); and most perplexing of all, the Trinity (Who were these three persons of the Godhead, how did they relate to one another, and how could they be explained as one God in the context of the polytheistic Roman culture?). But at the heart of their theology was the practice of prayer. They lived and wrote by the notion of *lex orandi, lex credendi*: out of the law of praying comes the law of belief. In short, we can know God by prayer. Evagrius, a desert monk in the fourth century, is often quoted: "A theologian is one who prays and one who prays is a theologian."[3] The very first creedal statements came out of liturgical practice: at baptism, converts were baptized in the name of the Father, the Son, and the Holy Spirit.

Ironically, patristic theology is often presented to us as undigested chunks of rather tricky doctrine. In this way, we have got the early church wrong. In the second century, Irenaeus wrote, "Our teaching is consonant with what we do in the Eucharist, and the Eucharist establishes what we teach."[4] Gregory of Nyssa, one of the most philosophical theologians of his time and much involved in controversies about the nature of the Trinity, writing in the late fourth century, criticized one of his enemies, Eunomius, for ignoring Christian practices and relying solely on Christian ideas. "It is foolish and idle to think that Christian faith exists only in teaching," he scolded. "[If one] thinks that Christianity consists solely in 'doctrinal precision,' the Christian mystery becomes a 'pious fable.'"[5] Such theologians challenge us to bring practice and doctrine together, always using practice as our starting point.

## Lenten Practice

Lent is traditionally a time for learning, preparation, and examination, not only for those wishing to join the Christian faith, but for all Christians. This book invites us to enter the Lenten practice of those early catechumens and to reflect on what a practical Christianity might look like in and for our lives.

Our focus in our Lenten practice is three-fold: we turn to look at our self and our life; at our relationship with God; and at our relationships with others.

First of all, Lent is a time for self-reflection and self-examination, and our model is Jesus, who took himself into the desert for forty days and forty nights to prepare himself spiritually and emotionally for his ministry, and for all that lay ahead of him. Secondly, it is a time for turning more consciously to God. We look at our prayer life, and the things in our lives that compete with God for our attention. We respond to our own thirst for God. Thirdly, we look outward, not only at our existing relationships, but also to see what our neighbor needs, and how we can respond to Jesus' call to serve and love.

This book considers these three practices, and invites the reader to examine each area or activity in turn, while recognizing that each will also be interrelated. Chapters 1 and 2 focus on the examination of self; they take the metaphor of dust, suggesting that we look at the dustiness, or sin, in our lives, how to shake it off, and what the practice of forgiveness and letting go may mean. These chapters are about preparing ourselves for living sanely in a messy world, or, to put it another way, equipping ourselves for a life of faith in a sinful world and being aware of our part in it all. As we move through these practices, we will flesh out the doctrines of creation, original sin, and forgiveness.

In chapters 3 and 4, we turn to our relationship with God. Chapter 3 is about faith and salvation and—paradoxically—the importance of doubt in a life of faith. Chapter 4 focuses on what we can see and know of God, especially in our prayer and worshipping life. The doctrine that undergirds this conversation is that of the Trinitarian Godhead—or the three distinct ways that God becomes known to us.

By chapter 5, we are ready to focus on love; in particular, how we demonstrate and practice our faith in reaching out to our neighbor and the wider world. At the same time, we explore love as a doctrine, observing the way Christians can understand our relationship with and responsibility in the world.

In the interest of remaining at once rooted in tradition and imminently practical, each chapter sets out at least one biblical passage for reflection, but also a poem or works of art. Each also ends with a set of questions to guide your individual reflections, and the discussions in a wider study group in your parish or worshipping community.

## A Practical Path

Lent is sometimes presented as a spiritual marathon, and this is mistaken. Lent is not a time of pointless hardship. It is not a case of giving up dessert simply to crave it and be miserable. Nor is it an obstacle course to some kind of unattainable perfection. Rather, the season of Lent offers an opportunity to create the conditions by which we can turn more regularly and with more discipline towards an examination of ourselves, turn to God and look outward. In that sense Lent is an entirely positive season.

One of my own Lenten practices is to re-read the letters of Evelyn Underhill, the early twentieth-century Anglican writer on prayer and mysticism. They are full of common sense: they remind me of the essential balance and order that emerges when one is properly focused on God. They are based in her own wrestling with God, her attempts to live a disciplined devotional life and her work with others. In a letter to one of her regular correspondents, she wrote, "As to your Lent—no physical hardships beyond what normal life provides—but take each of these as serenely and gratefully as you can and make of them your humble offerings to God. Don't reduce sleep. Don't get up in the cold. Practice more diligently the art of turning to God with some glance or phrase of love or trust at all spare moments of the day. . . . Be specially kind and patient with those who irritate you. . . . Instead of wasting energy in being disgusted with yourself, *accept* your own failures, and just say to God 'Well, in spite of all I may say or fancy, this is what I am really like—so please help my weakness.' This, not self-disgust, is the real and fruitful humility."[6]

Underhill also had the capacity to suggest, gently, alternative practices to the overly zealous. To another of her spiritual directees, who was always trying to take on strict ascetic practices, indeed deliberate mortifications, Underhill suggested "by preference the mortification of the Tongue. Careful guard on all amusing criticism of others, on all complaints however casual or trivial; deliberately refraining sometimes (*not* always!) from saying the entertaining thing. This does not mean you are to be dull or correct! but to ration this side of your life. I doubt whether things like sitting on the least comfortable chair, etc., affect you enough to be worth bothering about! But I'm sure custody of the Tongue (on the lines suggested) could give you quite a bit of trouble and be a salutary bit of discipline, a sort of verbal hair-shirt."[7]

Underhill also encouraged those who were struggling with certain doctrines to leave them on one side for a while, and focus on the practice of Christianity. She wrote to one enquirer: "As to dogmas which you cannot accept—e.g. the Virgin Birth—it is useless to force yourself on these points. Leave them alone for the time being, neither affirming nor rejecting them, and give your mind and will to living in harmony with those truths which you do see." She continued: "When you speak of reading more than practise in your life, you put your finger on a real source of spiritual weakness. You would benefit by a simple rule of life. . . . Leave the more doctrinal side alone for the present. And go humbly, taking no notice of how you 'feel.' This really matters very little!"[8]

There are more echoes with Underhill's work, especially with the small book entitled *Practical Mysticism*, in which she works out what mysticism might mean for the ordinary person. Mysticism was always a practical path for her. It was attainable by anyone because it could be learned. The result for anyone embracing the mystic way in the midst of their regular lives was, according to Underhill, "a larger and intenser life" that was "practical and affirmative; giving scope for a limitless activity of will, heart and mind working within the rhythms of the Divine Idea."[9]

Evelyn Underhill makes a number of appearances in this book, as do some other twentieth-century Christians, influential on my faith and thinking, who have now joined God's host of saints: Anthony Cardovo Campbell, Henry Chadwick, Verna Dozier, John Fenton, W.R. Inge, R.H. Lightfoot, and William Temple. They join in these pages with some contemporary practitioners and writers whose witness to God's love has also been inspirational to me: Marilyn McCord Adams, James Alison, Sara Miles, David Stancliffe, and Vincent Strudwick. I hope that after putting this book down, you may enjoy taking up the work of some of these people, as well as the novels of Philip Pullman, Donna Tartt, and Catherine Fox; the writings of Patricia Williams; the poems of Molly Peacock, Mary Oliver, Virginia Hamilton Adair, and Yehuda Amichai; the artwork of Grace Cossington Smith and John Olsen; and the music of Jimmy Scott; all of which have shaped my thinking and practice.

The point of this book is to help us imagine how Christian practice can transform our lives and the world around us, and by that practice how we may come to understand more fully the central beliefs or doctrines of Christianity. These doctrines need no longer seem alien or impossible; rather, they are ideas with which to grapple in the daily grain of our lives, providing us with a compelling vision of how the world transformed might be. And it is this that draws us into Christian community—not the desire to become a body of like-minded people compelled to believe and do exactly the same thing, but to become a group of diverse women and men who care about transforming themselves and the world by love.

## For Reflection

1. How would you answer the query put to the early catechumens: "How has your life been transformed by Christianity?" Is this a more difficult question than the alternative: "What do you believe?" Why or why not?

2. Can you think of an instance where the practice of Christianity has helped you more fully understand a doctrine?

3. How have you approached Lenten disciplines and practice in the past? Consider the words of Evelyn Underhill: "As to your Lent—no physical hardships beyond what normal life provides—but take each of these as serenely and gratefully as you can and make of them your humble offerings to God." How could this advice shape your Lenten journey?

The hand of the Lord was upon me, and he brought me out by the Spirit of the Lord, and set me down in the midst of the valley; it was full of bones. And he led me round among them; and behold, there were very many upon the valley; and lo, they were very dry. And he said to me, 'Son of man, can these bones live?' And I answered, 'O Lord God, thou knowest.' Again he said to me, 'Prophesy to these bones, and say to them, O dry bones, hear the word of the Lord. Thus says the Lord God to these bones: Behold, I will cause breath to enter you, and you shall live. And I will lay sinews upon you, and will cause flesh to come upon you, and cover you with skin, and put breath in you, and you shall live; and you shall know that I am the Lord.'

So I prophesied as I was commanded; and as I prophesied, there was a noise, and behold, a rattling; and the bones came together, bone to its bone. And as I looked, there were sinews on them, and flesh had come upon them, and skin had covered them; but there was no breath in them. Then he said to me, 'Prophesy to the breath, prophesy, son of man, and say to the breath, Thus says the Lord God: Come from the four winds, O breath, and breathe upon these slain, that they may live.' So I prophesied as he commanded me, and the breath came into them, and they lived, and stood upon their feet, an exceedingly great host.

Ezekiel 37:1–10 (RSV)

## The Problem of Dust

In Philip Pullman's powerfully imaginative novel *The Golden Compass*, dust drives the narrative and governs everything. Dust, in this novel, consists of particles from another world that cause knowledge—or, in theological language, original sin. The overriding intellectual quest, and the central battles in the book, are about discovering the origin and meaning of dust; and, for some of the characters in the book, about overcoming the power of dust and thus eliminating the existence of original sin, often via cruel means.

While Pullman would stoutly disavow any Christian belief, and the church comes off very badly in the book, the novel is in many ways a working out of a verse in Genesis 3: "From dust you have come, and to dust you shall return." This phrase, repeated in the Christian liturgy on Ash Wednesday, the first day of Lent, reminds us of our mortality. Traditionally, Christianity has used that reminder—when life was "nasty, brutish and short" as the seventeenth-century philosopher Thomas Hobbes put it—to speak of our immortality, to promise something better in a future life. But in the Western world today, where the material quality of life is so high for so many and life expectancy is long, it is not primarily the thought of a heavenly (or hellish) afterlife that determines our actions. Rather, we are guided by love, work, success, money, illness, relationships. Our lives are shaped by our attitudes to these things that preoccupy us here and now. To speak of dust, in this context, is to acknowledge our humble beginnings (literally as humus, or dirt) and discern what it means to lead a moral life, a good life, in a world beset by "dust" understood in a different but related sense, namely sin.

Pullman shares the church's commitment to the quest for the good life. But he would join many intelligent critics in saying that Christianity does not have a monopoly on morality. If anything, for Pullman, true morality must occur outside the limiting and damaging force of the institutional churches.

As a priest who for a long time worked in a university environment, my interest—shaped by my pastoral experience—has long been in this tension between those atheists and agnostics like Pullman who wish to shape a good and moral life, and a Christianity that has a choice to make: either to acknowledge or refute the credibility of such skepticism. And in my present ministry, as dean of a large cathedral on the west coast of the USA, I see that we face that same choice here, where so few people go to church—or indeed any place of worship. My own choice has always been to acknowledge the validity of that criticism, and then to find a place from within Christianity that may address the concerns of those on the margins of the church, outside and peering in, as well as those who are central to the church, but want something more, and thereby to demonstrate Christianity's particular contribution to shaping the "good life."

The questions then become, for Christians and non-Christians alike: what does Christianity offer us in this life? What does faith enable us to do and to be? Are there guiding principles in Christianity that can help us with our relationships, jealousies, and resentments; the knotty problems in our jobs or the desolation of unemployment or underemployment; exhaustion and overwork; and that fear of something—we are not always quite sure what—that keeps us awake at night? In short, how can the practice of a spiritual life help us with all those things which make daily living utterly real and often ugly and painful—our dust? And what particular resources and ideas does Christianity bring to such a life?

## The Most Democratic of Substances

Dust is a biblical metaphor, and it helpfully speaks to our beginnings and our endings, to our place in this world, to the life in Christ that Christians share, and to the practical means by which we may live our lives. In the second of the creation stories in which God makes humankind, it is said: "the Lord God formed man from the dust of the ground" (Genesis 2:7). Later in Genesis, God reminds human beings of their mortality in the words, "you are dust, and to dust you shall return" (Genesis 3:19). The philosopher Alain de Botton writes memorably, in his book *Status Anxiety*, that "Dust is that most democratic of substances."[10] It is the stuff from which we are all created.

This raises an existential question: if we all come from the same place, the same substance, and are reduced back to that substance at the end of our lives, what meaning do any of our achievements, our possessions, the things which we believe give us status (our jobs, children, the "right" address, the "right" house, an expensive car, entry into a particular social group) have? In the face of enormous social anxiety, Christianity forces us to realize, finally realize, that for all our achievements and riches, human beings are created equal, from the same substance, and, more than that, in the image and likeness of God.

Jesus himself was the one who reminded his followers that we are all equally and beautifully composed of dust. It was Jesus who washed the dust off his disciples' feet when they came for supper the night before he died (John 13:1–17).

This act turned the world upside down. Dust may be that most democratic of substances: it gets in all our toes if we walk on a dusty country road in sandals, as Jesus and his disciples did, day in, day out, so whenever they entered another's house their feet would be washed by servants or slaves. But to wash the dust off your disciples' feet in a deeply hierarchical society was to engage in a radically democratic act. From Jesus' acts—this and others—there resulted a radical egalitarianism, which was a hallmark of the earliest communities of Christians. In a society divided into slave and free, with a carefully delineated, hierarchical social system, and where women had no public role, Christians provided an alternative. Christians of all sorts ate and worshipped together in the same room, and attempted to assign offices within their churches (priest, bishop, deacon, prophet) according to gifts, not rank, gender, or whether a person was a free person or a slave. Paul expressed it like this, in his letter to the Galatians in the first century: "There is no longer Jew or Greek, there is no longer slave or free, there is no longer male or female; for all of you are one in Christ Jesus" (Galatians 3:28).

This sort of radical egalitarianism stood in stark contrast with the wider society where women and men, slave and free, would never have sat in the same room together to eat. Christians were therefore described by the pagans in the following sorts of terms. Here the early Latin Christian apologist, Minucius, constructs a dialogue between a pagan and a Christian, and the pagan says that the Christians "are a gang of discredited and proscribed desperadoes. . . . They have gathered together from the lowest dregs of the populace ignorant men and credulous women—and women are naturally unstable—and formed a rabble of impious conspirators."[11]

For the pagan philosophers, a group that attracted women or the other "dregs" of society had little merit: in a world where rank mattered, it was the number of educated male disciples and followers you had that counted. Christianity shattered that presupposition, and consequently Christians thought of themselves as resident aliens in the Roman Empire. Washing the dust off the feet of those who were, in societal terms, deemed lower than you was part of a startling and liberating movement.

Whatever the churches have made of Jesus, the radical rabbi of the first century, he emerges from the pages of the gospels as a man whose ethical teaching based in love and the basic equality of all human beings in the eyes of God was and is highly attractive. Here was a man who healed on the Sabbath because he wished people to be well and to flourish, rather than adhering needlessly to the law; who spoke to the woman at the well even though she was of "bad" reputation; who sat and ate with the hated tax collectors; who touched dead bodies when it was utterly taboo to do so—and brought them back to life; who honored the woman who poured expensive oil over him and thereby "chrismated" him (named him as the Christ in an act of devotion) when all around him grumbled. Here, too, was the man who washed his disciples' feet with care, embracing their dust and shattering notions of high or low, clean or unclean, worthy or unworthy.

## Grappling with Sin

In Pullman's novel *The Golden Compass* and the following two books in the trilogy of which it is a part, the misguided characters, such as Mrs. Coulter (played so compellingly by Nicole Kidman in the film version), try to destroy dust, believing that to live a good life we have to get rid of our created nature, and especially original sin. In their attempts to get rid of dust, they cause immense pain and suffering.

For some, the notion of a paradise to which we might return, or which we might build on earth, is a way of escaping the dust of our lives; it promises an escape from sin. Utopian communities—both religious and secular—stand as a testament to human beings' capacity for imagining a brighter future and for deluding themselves. The whole idea of modern society's progress was something of a utopian dream, shattered by World War I and the later atrocities of the twentieth century.

In Pullman's work, the central characters Lyra and Will learn that the moral life, the good life, is not lived in a dust-free vacuum but is rather lived out in the quest, in the journey and in the choices that one makes in a complex world filled with pain and suffering as well as joy and hope. If we cannot eradicate dust and sin, there must be an alternative path, some way to grapple with our faults, shake off the effects and continue on the journey.

In the language and practice of the church, this process of letting go is done through the sacrament of reconciliation: namely, confession and repentance. The first stage is always stating things as they are: What do we need to confess? What is the dust of sin in our lives that we need to acknowledge in order that we can shake it off? Unless we make that acknowledgment, we cannot move on, and this is true of both our personal or individual sins, and collective or institutional sins, although of course these are often interrelated.

Patricia Williams, the legal theorist, writes of the ways we as a society need to acknowledge racism—what I as a

Christian would call the sin of racism—in order that we can confront it and be reconciled. We might wish for a color-blind society, and many do, but we must first account for who we are and what we do. As Williams puts it, "It is a dangerous if comprehensible temptation to imagine inclusiveness by imagining away any obstacles. . . . [T]he moral high ground of good intentions [has] its limits. We must be careful not to allow our intention to verge into outright projection by substituting a fantasy of global seamlessness that is blinding rather than just color-blind."[12] In other words, wishing that all is well does not make everything well. There is grappling and reconciling work to do.

Our Lenten discipline begins by kneeling at the altar rail and having the priest mark our foreheads with ash, reminding us that we have come from dust, and we will go back to dust. We share the Lenten litany, in which we state collectively what we have done that was wrong, and what we have left undone. The forty days that follow provide a dedicated opportunity for personal examination, and in our churches and worshipping communities they may allow a space for collective reflection and examination, too. Along with Williams, we have to acknowledge the limits to "the moral high ground of good intentions." God wants us to be more than our human limits, and with God's help we can be, but we have to know what those limits are. That is a spiritual practice.

Jesus once again guides our practice. He sent his disciples out to preach God's love and commanded them to shake the dust off their feet on leaving any village where they were not welcome. (See Mark 6:11; Luke 9:5 and 10:11; Matthew 10:14.) His words stand out as common sense of the highest order. For me, this practical advice encourages disciples to release bitterness and forgive those who have wronged them, a practice we will take up in the next chapter. But it also inspires them—and us—to do the work of self-examination, to discern where we continually fall short and recognize how our dustiness prevents our living freely and fully.

For several years in England there was a BBC reality television program called *Life Laundry*; in the U.S., there was a similar series called *Clean Sweep* on The Learning Channel. In this program, people with very cluttered and messy houses who cannot stop collecting old comic books or garden statues or hoarding broken washing machines that they might mend one day, or something else utterly useless, or who simply cannot throw anything out, submit themselves—on television, which never ceases to amaze me—to a very bossy woman and her slightly timid male sidekick who go through their houses, telling them what to keep and what to throw out. There is a bit of pop psychology thrown in along the way about why the homeowners accumulated so much rubbish.

My hope is that we might all gain the spiritual tools for ourselves—without a bossy television presenter coming into our houses—to do a bit of "life laundry," not just about material objects but all the difficult situations and relationships which accumulate in our lives and cause us embarrassment or upset or grief or resentment. One session of *Life Laundry* from someone else does not do it: my guess is that those houses get cluttered all over again once the television cameras have left. We need to learn the spiritual tools for ourselves to keep on discerning throughout our lives what to wrestle with, what to let go of, and how with God's grace to re-engage to effect a transformation. We all have dustiness, limits, sin, and eventually the only course is to deal with it.

## Life after Dust

The point of reckoning with the reality of dust—coming to accept our created nature, including the flaws—is to move towards and embrace life in all its fullness. God longs to bring us to new life despite our limitations, for there are no limitations with God. Out of our dust, through the clouds of dust that we shake off, comes new life. This is marvelously depicted in our biblical passage: Ezekiel 37:1-10.

> The hand of the Lord was upon me, and he brought me out by the Spirit of the Lord, and set me down in the midst of the valley; it was full of bones. And he led me round among them; and behold, there were very many upon the valley; and lo, they were very dry. And he said to me, "Son of man, can these bones live?" And I answered, "O Lord God, thou knowest." Again he said to me, "Prophesy to these bones, and say to them, O dry bones, hear the word of the Lord. Thus says the Lord God to these bones: Behold, I will cause breath to enter you, and you shall live. And I will lay sinews upon you, and will cause flesh to come upon you, and cover you with skin, and put breath in you, and you shall live; and you shall know that I am the Lord."
>
> So I prophesied as I was commanded; and as I prophesied, there was a noise, and behold, a rattling; and the bones came together, bone to its bone. And as I looked, there were sinews on them, and flesh had come upon them, and skin had covered them; but there was no breath in them. Then he said to me, "Prophesy to the

breath, prophesy, son of man, and say to the
breath, Thus says the Lord God: Come from the
four winds, O breath, and breathe upon these
slain, that they may live." So I prophesied as
he commanded me, and the breath came into
them, and they lived, and stood upon their feet,
an exceedingly great host.

Ezekiel is brought to a valley of dusty, dry bones and
God commands him to prophesy to the bones so that they
might live. It seems an impossible task. But Ezekiel follows
God's instructions, prophesying that God's breath might
enter the dry bones. The dry bones begin to rattle and shake
as they miraculously take on first flesh and then life, so that
a vast multitude of people comes to stand before Ezekiel in
the valley, where before there had simply been bones. This
vast multitude is a sign to the people of Israel—in exile at this
point—that life can come out of their spiritual aridity, their
despair and despondency.

Here our verse from Genesis 3 is turned upside down.
What the Ezekiel story suggests is this: you shall go back to
dust, but by the mighty power of an all-loving God, from
dust you shall be given new life. We may all be formed from
dust and return to dust, but there is hope: the belief that God
is a God of life and flourishing, not of death and decay. God
always wants us to come to fullness of life, to be wholly who
we are called to be, dust and all.

What, then, does Christianity bring to the quest for
a moral life, the struggle to live with our dustiness? The
promise that we are created of dust *and* in the image of God,
and that we will be accompanied in our journey by the love
of God, a love greater than our sin, greater than our limits.

## For Reflection

1. Consider the phrase: "From dust you have come, and to dust you shall return." In what ways do these words comfort you? In what ways do they challenge you?

2. In many church services, there is very little silence for reflection following the invitation to confession. What is so difficult about confession or saying "I'm sorry," especially in public?

3. If you did a "life laundry" exercise, what would you need to confess or release about your life, your habits, your choices?

4. Where do you see glimmers of new life, dry bones taking on flesh? Where do you wish to see new life?

CHAPTER 2

# Letting Go

[Jesus] called the twelve and began to send them out two by two, and gave them authority over the unclean spirits. He ordered them to take nothing for their journey except a staff; no bread, no bag, no money in their belts; but to wear sandals and not to put on two tunics. He said to them, "Wherever you enter a house, stay there until you leave the place. If any place will not welcome you and they refuse to hear you, as you leave, shake off the dust from your feet when you leave, as a testimony against them."

*Mark 6:7–11 (and compare Luke 9:1–6; Luke 10:1–11; Matthew 10:5–14)*

About fifty years ago, a jazz singer named Jimmy Scott looked set to make his big break. He was being much lauded in jazz circles, and people were certain he would become a star like Frank Sinatra. His voice was unusual because he suffered from Kellman's Syndrome, a hormone deficiency which stunted his growth and meant that his voice had an extraordinary quality—that of a boy's voice before it has broken mixed with the maturity of a grown man's experience. It was often compared with the voice of the female jazz singer Billie Holiday.

In 1963 he recorded the album that everyone said would make him a household name. And then there was a difficulty with the contract, and the album was pulled while Jimmy Scott was away on his honeymoon. Though he did continue to sing, Jimmy Scott spent most of the rest of his working life as an elevator operator and shipping clerk in a hotel in Cincinnati, Ohio. He began to make a comeback in the 1990s and then, in 2003, forty years after it was made, that album from 1963, *Falling in Love Again*, was brought out to all the critical acclaim that it might have received in the sixties.

I remember hearing Jimmy Scott being interviewed on the radio that year, and being struck by the fact that he showed no bitterness, no resentment, only delight that the album was being re-released. Asked if he ever thought this day would come, he said, "Well, I always had hope."

When rejection and disappointment happened, Jimmy Scott was not defeated or bitter, nor did he point fingers and blame his record label and batter away for the fame he was entitled to. He shook the dust off his feet, made a different life for himself and he retained his hope. And when his old jazz album came out, when he was seventy-eight years old, he was simply grateful. Or as he put it, "You know, after you get on, well, what's the grudge for? What's the hate for? You live on and on with that anger and that hate in you, and it takes effect. You have to use a little wisdom and a little understanding. And I'm not the only person in the world that's happened to. What, I'm gonna sit and cry by myself?"

Jesus says to his disciples, "If any place will not welcome you and they refuse to hear you, as you leave, shake off the dust from your feet when you leave, as a testimony against them." This is one of the most useful pieces of advice Jesus gives to his disciples—and so to us. It's that little bit of wisdom and understanding that Jimmy Scott speaks of—and it can make the difference between a life of bitterness and a life of joy.

## *Shaking the Dust off Your Feet*

Jesus' injunction to his disciples to shake the dust off their feet occurs in all three of the synoptic gospels. It comes just as he sends the twelve out on a short mission, to preach repentance and heal. As Mark and Luke tell the story, the disciples all come back together again quite soon for the feeding of the five thousand (the great miracle story that comes later in the chapter). Luke has two versions of this story—one with the twelve disciples, one just a little later with seventy being sent out.

Biblical commentators have varying opinions on what the exhortation to shake the dust off their feet may mean. Many see a judgment on the towns who have rejected the disciples' message. The sixteenth-century Protestant reformer John Calvin, for example, speaks of "a heavy sanction of punishment" striking "fear upon the rebellious" and says that Jesus "orders the Apostles to be the spokesman of that vengeance which He pronounces." Calvin hazards a guess that "to 'shake off the dust' was probably a usage of the Jews of those days, a sign of anathema . . ." and "a form of curse."[13] More recent biblical scholars are not so sure. The Anglican biblical scholar C. F. Evans has instead proposed that the gesture of the feet as a testimony against the town suggests "a prophetic sign by which the missionaries disclaim further responsibility."[14] Whatever happens from here on, they have done what they came to do and now it is in God's hands.

To best understand this text, I think we need to see the human Jesus, the compassionate man who gives practical instructions to the disciples based on his own experience. Why does Jesus offer this advice to his disciples? Perhaps the answer is simple: because he has been rejected over and over again, and he is preparing his friends for that experience. Jesus sends his followers out in the middle of his own mission and ministry of healing and teaching—a mission in which he has experienced repeated rejection, hostility, and cynicism.

Mark situates this story just after Jesus had taught in his hometown of Nazareth, where the people took such offense that he could do just about nothing there and had to leave. Jesus was, Mark tells us, amazed at their unbelief. Mark's placement of the story conjures up an image of Jesus stumbling out of the town where he grew up, scarcely able to believe that his own neighbors and friends, the people who have watched him grow up, have refused to believe or accept him. The rejection is fresh and raw, and yet he keeps on going. He continues his ministry, traveling about the villages, teaching and healing. So when he sends his disciples out, he knows that they too will be rejected, and he passes on wisdom for how to deal with it.

We all experience rejection and disappointment: the big

rejections like the end of a relationship or not getting a job we want, and the smaller, daily rejections, too—someone we care for ignores us or a respected colleague rejects our contribution. Jesus' advice to his disciples equips them for a different way of life, a way that is free of disillusionment, bitterness, and resentment in the face of rejections and disappointments. Shake the dust off your feet and move on.

## Giving Our Hurt to God

What do we need for this? At one level, absolutely nothing. Jesus tells his disciples to take nothing with them on their mission: no bread, no bag, no money in their belt, no change of tunic. We are exhorted to travel light, literally and metaphorically. This applies to the whole of Christian life. In some very basic way, we need nothing. Why? Because God loves us exactly as we are, unconditionally. This is the extraordinary promise of the Christian gospel.

But leading a life in which we truly accept God's love of us and of others is neither intuitive nor easy. We all know how appealing it can be to nurse a grievance against someone who slighted us yesterday or a week ago, or a year ago, or ten years ago. Filled with indignation or self-pity, we just know that we are right! And a little rock of bitterness grows in our heart.

We have to *learn* how to shake the dust off our feet, when so much else in society tells us not to. In the last chapter, I evoked the *Life Laundry* program. Now I am thinking of the myriad television programs that encourage us to fester in our resentment: programs about neighbors from hell—people who hate their neighbors because of the big tree in their garden, or people punching and confronting each other on *The Jerry Springer Show*. We live in an increasingly litigious culture, in which people are more frequently invited to sue each other than to sort out problems and move on. Discerning when to let go spiritually or when to persist with something is a vital part of the Christian life. Indeed, letting go of the hurt of rejection is often what enables us to go on with our lives with hope and faith. Numerous medical studies tell us that letting go of resentments, anger, thoughts of revenge and grudges, all lead not only to spiritual health but also to emotional and physical health.

Shaking the dust off our feet leads to that place of health and peace. Letting go in this way requires letting God deal with that which we find difficult. For the disciples, shaking the dust off their feet as they leave a town that has rejected their message is about leaving the matter between the town and God. It is no longer their business; they have other towns to visit, other places to go and preach. The focus, in the biblical text, remains on the interior life of the disciple, rather than on the villagers.

So, with us, once we have truly let go of that painful situation at work or a destructive relationship or a resentment against someone who (we think) has done us wrong, the matter is left for God to deal with. We get on with our own God-given tasks, using our own God-given gifts to positive effects: in short, continue to develop who we are called to be by God, to flourish, rather than pouring our energy into destructive situations and relationships. In this way, we learn to rejoice in all things, great and small, to accept God's love of us and in turn, to love one another as Christ loves us.

Jimmy Scott, the jazz singer, put it like this: "I grew to see my affliction as my gift. When I sang, I soared. I could soar higher than all those hurts aimed at my heart. . . . It's been an inspirational growth for me—to keep that spirit going and be inspired to continue to work. You just don't get to a point and say I give up!" When we give a difficult situation over to God, God's grace can enter and transformation can occur. Jimmy Scott certainly did not expect his album to be released forty years after he made it, but he remained open to possibility.

New life in Christ means waking up each day having shaken off the dust and debris of our own sins and the harm that others have done us—and knowing new life is always possible. Go forward, unencumbered, into a new day, says Jesus. In shaking the dust off our feet, we leave things with God. Knocking that dust off our feet is a symbolic representation of the inward process of turning the issue completely back to God.

## *The Hope for Transformation*

Sometimes God's grace requires us to take up hard work, to re-engage with a difficult situation in a completely different way. Shirley Chisholm was the first black woman in Congress. In 1972, George Wallace, Alabama's white governor who had been against civil rights, was made disabled in an assassination attempt. This was in the middle of Chisholm's presidential campaign. Chisholm visited him in hospital and later said rather ruefully, "Black people in my community crucified me. But why shouldn't I go to visit him? Every other presidential candidate was going to see him. He said to me, 'What are your people going to say?' I said: 'I know what they're going to say. But I wouldn't want what happened to you to happen to anyone.' He cried and cried and cried."

Chisolm always believed her action brought beneficial long-term consequences. After he had recovered enough to return to politics, Wallace attempted to make some amends for his opposition to African-American attempts to gain civil rights. Several years later, Chisolm worked on a bill to give domestic workers the right to a minimum wage, and Wallace helped gain votes of enough Southern congressmen to get the legislation through the U.S. House of Representatives.[15]

This story reminds us that sometimes we will need to let go of our resentments and bitterness and then re-engage with those who have caused them, all in order to effect (with God's grace) a transformation within a relationship. Such acts are not always popular with those around us, many of whom will surely think we have betrayed them or our own cause. Chisholm's choice of language is particularly telling: "My community crucified me," she said. The days before Jesus' crucifixion are full of actions like this—the enactment of his command "to love your enemies, do good to those who hate you, bless those who curse you, pray for those who abuse you" (Luke 6:27) and turn the other cheek. On the night before his death, Jesus kisses Judas who, he knows, will betray him and unleash the process that will lead to his crucifixion (Mark 14:44). Before Caiaphas, the high priest, he remains silent (Matthew 26:62–63). In the face of questioning from Pilate, he does not answer with bitterness about what has happened to him, nor does he self-righteously try to justify the actions on his part that have brought him to this point; he merely turns back onto Pilate what Pilate has said (John 19:26–27). On the cross, he does not waste time pouring scorn on his enemies, but takes care of his mother and the beloved disciple, entrusting them to each other's care. And in his final moments of life, strung up on the cross, he begs, "Father, forgive them for they know not what they do" (Luke 23:24).

In Jesus' life and in our own, letting go precipitates transformation, healing, and resurrection.

The possibilities of true forgiveness can be both shocking and life-giving. In the opera *The Last Supper* by the contemporary composer Harrison Birtwhistle, performed for the first time in the year 2000, the twelve apostles are called together for a second final supper in our own day. Jesus appears amongst them and then Judas walks in; the other disciples are shocked and horrified. But Jesus embraces him, wipes the red dust of the road off his feet, his clothes, his body, and weeps over the horrors perpetrated by humankind in the last two thousand years, most especially the Holocaust. Jesus sings to the other disciples, "Who is the betrayer? Who is the betrayed?" With these words he forces the eleven disciples to re-admit Judas to the group. They enter the garden, the cock crows, and the opera ends. It is a powerful piece of art, reminding us that there are no limits to the depths of our forgiveness. Our capacity to forgive correlates to our experience of new life.

When Peter went to Jesus and asked him how many times he should forgive someone who had done him wrong, supplying the answer of seven times within his question, Jesus replied "Not seven times, but, I tell you, seventy times" (Matthew 18:21–22). Jesus emphasizes the importance of forgiveness throughout the gospels. He taught his listeners that they needed to forgive others that they might be forgiven by God (Mark 11:25) and that they needed to make peace with their brothers and sisters before they came to worship (Matthew 5:24). The risen Christ breathed on his disciples and said: "Receive the Holy Spirit. If you forgive anyone their sins, they are forgiven; if you do not forgive them, they are not forgiven" (John 20:22–23, NIV). The theme returns in the

Acts of the Apostles and in many of the epistles. It is one of the most consistent teachings in the New Testament.

## *How Not to Forgive*

Many people remain—understandably—unable to forgive those who have committed an atrocity that has affected their lives deeply, such as killing or maiming loved ones in a terrorist attack or the violence of war. In an address broadcast on BBC Radio on Good Friday 2011, the Archbishop of Canterbury Rowan Williams warned that urging people towards easy forgiveness can make suffering appear not to matter. Williams said: "I think the twentieth century saw such a level of atrocity that it has focused our minds very, very hard on the dangers of forgiving too easily . . . because if forgiveness is easy it is as if the suffering doesn't really matter."[16] Those who work in the areas of restorative justice and reconciliation know how hard this work of forgiving can be. The Forgiveness Project, based in Britain, was founded by Marina Cantacuzino in response to the war in Iraq. She was dismayed by the rhetoric of "if you're not with us, you're against us." The project chronicles in words and pictures the difficult task of reconciliation between perpetrators and victims as part of its aim to help build a future free of conflict and violence by healing the wounds of the past. It hopes, by sharing stories of forgiveness and reconciliation at local, national, and international levels, that it can encourage people to explore the nature of forgiveness and alternatives to revenge.[17]

The theologian James Alison warns us that it is also quite possible to get forgiveness wrong. It is easy to make it an accusatory and compulsory act, something the wronged person demands. This becomes a sanctimonious and resentful demand for an apology. But forgiveness does not work like that. If God has always already forgiven us, just as God accepts us on the journey of faith exactly as who and where we are, then forgiveness of one human being by another must be like that too, for the sake of both parties. Or to put it another way, forgiveness starts long before anyone who is being forgiven knows what is going on. That is what Jesus was doing for us on the cross. And if the spiritual life is about the imitation of Christ, then our forgiveness of another is a free gesture that begins before the perpetrator says sorry. Indeed, the apology may surprise us. And in turn, being forgiven—discovering that something you seek has already been freely given—is a surprise.

Both parties, the forgiver and the forgiven, experience in this a certain vulnerability, a breaking apart of oneself, which seems impossible within the regime of a tightly ordered and controlled life, but is possible when we live in the love of God. Indeed, a sign of forgiving and being forgiven is this "breaking apart," the breaking open of our hearts: there is a reason for the expression "hard heartedness." There are no hard certainties here, no accusatory tones. It is the place from which new growth can happen. We experience what James Alison calls "the joy of being wrong."

Alison echoes these themes throughout his work. In his book *Faith Without Resentment*, he writes of wanting to create within the reader "something like a space in which a heart might find permission to come close to cracking." He calls this "a space which I am discovering to be necessary for participation in theological discourse" and goes on to explain:

[T]his closeness-to-cracking comes upon us at a moment when we do not know how to speak well, when we find ourselves threatened by confusion. It is where the two principal temptations are to bluster our way out of the moment, by speaking with too much security or arrogance so as to give the impression that the confusion is not mine, but belongs somewhere else. Or on the other hand to plunge into the shamed silence of one who knows himself uncovered, and for that reason deprived of legitimate speech. This space of the heart-close-to-cracking, poorly as it seems to promise, and difficult though it be to remain in it once it is found and occupied, seems to me the most appropriate way forward.[18]

He cites as an example of this Saul's conversion: an instance of the joy of being wrong. It means being unbound from our idols, allowing our sacred world to crumble, so that we can see God. In this sense, theology—new life—comes out of the dust of that crumbling, that cracking.

But Alison also warns us against using forgiveness as self-righteousness. This is why, as he repeatedly reminds us, we have to begin with ourselves as forgiven, as the recipients of forgiveness—not someone who is primarily a victim and secondly a forgiver, but primarily forgiven. That is what opens up our hearts, so that we can acknowledge hurts and wrongs, our own and another's (letting go of our hurts and resentments is not sweeping them under the carpet), the whole while knowing that all of our human mess is redeemed by God's love.

James Alison suggests that we are embarking on the

dangerous adventure of allowing ourselves to become forgiveness in imitation of the one who gave himself for us long before we knew we needed forgiving. That does not mean taking the moral high ground over and against the other party, but, rather, sticking with the other, inhabiting their universe, recognizing that we share the same mental and emotional properties. In the best of cases, knowing we are forgiven and forgiving, the breaking open of our hearts leads to some form of reconciliation, though not always. But it does always free us.

Knowing we are forgiven is about being free (and freed). Engaging in the act of forgiving is also about being free (and freed). It often seems easier to judge, regulate, and resent. But it is actually freeing when we discover we do not have to do any of that. We often do not want to forgive people, but we do want to be free. Freedom from our resentments leads us to living without fear. And we all want that.

Molly Peacock, who has worked as the poet-in-residence at the Cathedral of St. John the Divine in New York, writes this poem to conjure up just that feeling:

> Forgiveness is not an abstraction for
> it needs a body to feel its relief.
> Knees, shoulders, spine are required to adore
> the lightness of a burden removed. Grief,
> like a journey over water completed,
> slides its keel in the packed sand reef.
> Forgiveness is contact with the belief
> that your only life must now be lived. Knees
> once sank into the leather of the pew with all

the weight of created hell, of whom you did
   not ease,
or what you did not seize. Now the shortfall
that crippled your posture finds sudden peace
in the muscular, physical brightness
of a day alive: the felt lightness
of existence self-created, forgiveness.[19]

This experience of knowing we are forgiven is a physical thing. We *feel* the breaking apart in our bodies and our
souls, that true breaking apart which leads to a true knitting
together of us and God and our fellow human beings, and
thus to life at its fullest.

## For Reflection

1. What grievance do you wish you could forgive, but cannot? What are the circumstances? What holds you back?

2. Identify some practical ways that you could "give your hurts to God."

3. Is there any situation in which you believe people should not forgive those who have harmed them? Have you seen forgiveness backfire or not bring about healing?

4. Have you ever hurt someone and not been forgiven? What was the impact on you?

CHAPTER 3

# Being Uncertain

*When it was noon, darkness came over the whole land until three in the afternoon. At three o'clock Jesus cried out with a loud voice, "Eloi, eloi, lema sabachthani?" which means, "My God, my God, why have you forsaken me?"*

Mark 15:33–34

## The Problem with Certainty

Yehuda Amichai, a German-born Jew who moved to Israel in 1936 when he was eleven years old, knew first-hand the dangers of too much certainty. He explores them in his poem "The Place Where We Are Right."

From the place where we are right
    flowers will never grow
    in the spring.
The place where we are right
    is hard and trampled
    like a yard.
But doubts and loves
    dig up the world
    like a mole, a plow,
And a whisper will be heard in the place
    where the ruined
    house once stood.[20]

Writer Donna Tartt tells a story of the same harsh rightness, this certainty gone wrong, in her novel *The Little Friend*.[21] Harriet, the little girl who is the protagonist of the story, sets out to avenge her brother Robin's murder, long unsolved, a brooding force over her slowly unraveling family. Urged by the Baptist Sunday school teacher to do something useful in the summer vacation—a used car salesman, he has just been to a motivational sales conference and passes on the tips he has learned to the children in his Sunday school class—Harriet decides that she needs to do something more than win the library reading competition for yet another summer. She chooses the man she thinks was Robin's murderer and goes after him relentlessly with no thought that she is anything but right. Listening to the grown-ups around her, researching the crime in her local library's newspaper archive, and left to her own devices by an absent father and a mother undone by grief, she puts two and two together and makes five, and determines to put things right.

She pursues her goal without any thought for the consequences of her actions, mirroring an adult society that goes after the accused in the same way. The disastrous consequences of Harriet's grim task, as she crosses the tracks and enters a grown-up world of poverty and crime, reflect—for example—our own society's trial by media of those accused but not yet convicted. The logic of Harriet's actions is that a sacrifice must be made for the death of her brother and the subsequent disintegration of her family life.

There is a version of Christian theology that has this logic and demands this certainty too, and it relates in particular to what happened on Good Friday. It goes like this: God had a master plan. It was to restore the covenant with a sinful people. For that, someone had to be sacrificed to take away our sins. That someone was God's son, sent to earth to die for us. This was the required atonement to appease an austere and unforgiving God.

Many Christians put this theology at the center of their faith. Indeed, for many Christians, being saved depends entirely on the acceptance of this particular story in this particular form. In that tradition, salvation is equated with certainty, and faith is understood as having an unquestioning acceptance of a set of doctrines, particularly this version of the doctrine of atonement.

Certainty is appealing. The American theologian and Episcopalian Verna Dozier wrote beautifully about the "great human need for definite answers" and its dangers. She wrote:

We resist living with the doubt, incompleteness, confusion and ambiguity that are inescapable parts of the life we are called to live. Living by faith means living by unsureness. We cannot bear the uncertainties with which the gospel message calls us to live. We cannot bear having to take a risk that this is the way to go. We cannot bear our inability to know absolutely. So we hurry up and create some certainties that will relieve us of that anxiety.[22]

But where, in a theology of certainty, is there space for the cry, "My God, my God, why hast thou forsaken me?" Where is the space for the spontaneous grace and love poured out to a fellow human being, sharing the same grisly death on a cross on a hillside? Where, in that theology, is the angry Jesus who turned over the tables in the temple, and risked the wrath of those who had the power to kill him, because he wanted mercy and love, not commerce and profit, to be the hallmarks of our worship?

That theology of certainty takes away the riskiness of God's incarnation, of God's entry into the world as a vulnerable baby, of God's sharing our suffering. It ducks the sheer abundance of God's love.

## *The Cost of Christian Certainty*

Christian history is littered with examples of Christians being so certain that they were right that they separated from one another, persecuted one another, and even killed one another, moments when the strongest of ties became the most acrimonious of splits. As the distinguished church historian Henry Chadwick put it: "Religion when shared is one of the strongest of social bonds. When differences appear whether of rite or calendar or social custom or liturgy, or, above all, basic allegiance, this powerful bonding becomes counterproductive and easily engenders deep divisions."[23]

Our current churches are not immune from this temptation. For those of us who are Episcopalians and Anglicans, we all know that the Anglican Communion is beset by differences, disagreements, divisions, and mean-spirited threats of schism. It is a sorry tale: those coming after us will see it for what it is. Likewise, when we look back, we can get some perspective on the trivial nature of most of the disagreements that have caused division in our church. We should remember that people threatened to split the Church of England over the issue of candles on the altar, and other matters of ritual, in the early twentieth century.

In the last book he published before he died, Chadwick elucidated the reasons for the greatest split in Christendom of all: that between East and West, which came to a head in the eleventh century (in 1054) after a many-centuries-long buildup. The reasons for that split are of course many, but as Chadwick explains, some areas of dispute seem trivial to us now. One area of dispute was the question of beards: should monks and clergy have beards? In the East, yes; in the West, no. Christians in the East and West also quarreled over the nature of the bread to be used at communion: should it be unleavened or not? Of course that related to a deeper issue concerning the relation of the old and new covenants under the Christian dispensation. (The Greeks argued that to use unleavened bread was not obeying the Lord's will because it did not reflect the fact that the Lord's Supper was an inauguration of the new covenant.)

More famously, or perhaps infamously, there were sharp

differences about the nature of the Trinitarian Godhead. Was the Spirit equal with the Father and the Son? Did the Spirit proceed just from the Father or from the Father and the Son? These were the sorts of questions over which there was much bitter disagreement.[24] Here we have an example of two major branches of the Christian church disagreeing to the endpoint of schism on something ultimately unknowable: the precise nature of the Godhead.

If I asked you to describe God, what would you say? If Jesus walked in your church door, would you recognize him?

At the Transfiguration—that glorious moment on the mountain when Jesus' divinity is revealed—his disciples are confused. Those closest to him fail to recognize that divinity, his identity. They respond with confusion, fear, foolish suggestions. This is who we are: the confused, the ones who don't understand, who look in the wrong direction when God is underneath our noses. And yet we dare to disagree with each other on the grounds that we think we know exactly what God wants or does not want, exactly who God is and is not. In short, we human beings lack humility.

## Uncertainty in the Gospel of Mark

There is a tradition within Christianity that suggests that God is so beyond our human understanding that we cannot ever know God, and it is only by acknowledging this that we can know God. This is called the *via negativa*, or the negative way. We can apprehend God only by not apprehending God. God is to be affirmed as the cause of everything, and yet no affirmation is adequate for God. It is only by these paradoxes that we will go beyond our narrow, inadequate, all-too-human frames of reference for God.

We find this approach in the writings of theologians such as Denys (or Dionysus) the Areopagite in the early sixth century, and John of the Cross, one of the great mystics of the sixteenth century. Denys, for example, says God is so utterly different from creation, we cannot say anything accurate about God. God is both being itself and the source of all being; God is the Nameless One with many names; we speak of the attributes of the One who is beyond all attribution. These denials (the apophatic approach, to use the technical term) get us closer to God than the affirmations, says Denys. This is a very impersonal view of God, and it is not true to the full Christian tradition, but it can provide an important corrective to a particular sort of religious sensibility which believes that it knows everything there is to know about God, and that any other view of God is wrong.[25]

Some would say this negative tradition began with the Gospel of Mark, and here I have been much influenced by the work of the British New Testament scholar John Fenton, and his teacher, R. H. Lightfoot, who was one of my predecessors as Dean of Divinity at New College, Oxford. Mark's is a strange gospel: it has no birth story; it has rather a shortage of Jesus' teaching (no sermon on the mount—that comes in Matthew; no sermon on the plain—that comes in Luke; no Lord's Prayer), no resurrection appearance, and no words of glory at the end. Jesus says very little to Pilate, quite unlike the Jesus in John's gospel who turns the questioning around onto his interrogator. Even those who are crucified with Jesus taunt him in Mark's gospel. On the cross, Jesus says, "My God, my God, why hast thou forsaken me?" The gospel ends on a note of despair. The disciples have failed and they have fled. Peter has denied Jesus at the end of chapter 14 of the gospel, and that is the last we hear of him. The women who go to the tomb are afraid when they find it empty and say nothing to anyone about what they have seen.

The original ending of the gospel is a little less than halfway through the final chapter, at chapter 16, verse 8: the women have gone to the tomb on Sunday morning with oils to anoint the body. They arrive and find the stone rolled back; a young man (an angel?) tells them, "Fear nothing, you are looking for Jesus of Nazareth, who was crucified. He has been raised again; he is not here." They are commanded to give a message to the male disciples: that the risen Jesus has gone into Galilee where "you will see him, as he told you," but the women, despite being told to fear nothing, do the exact opposite—they run away from the tomb. "Beside themselves with terror . . . they said nothing to anybody, for they were afraid." To the very end of this gospel, human beings are presented as full of fear, failure, and weakness.

R. H. Lightfoot was one of the first people in English biblical scholarship to suggest that Mark really did mean to end the gospel halfway through what we know as chapter 16, with these words: "They said nothing to anybody for they were afraid." This was radical when he first proposed it in England in 1938; scholars believed that the author of the gospel intended to proceed further but was prevented from doing so, or had written more but that the last part of that chapter had been quickly lost. No one seriously believed that the author intentionally ended his work at that negative verse. But Lightfoot made the case, and while his work was regarded as highly unusual at the time, scholars have largely come to accept that the last twelve verses of Mark's gospel—in which the risen Lord appears to the male disciples—were added at a later date.[26]

So Mark's telling of the story is a sad one. It ends on a note of rejection, condemnation, and fear. Why? Is it because Mark intends to unsettle us, raising questions which take away an arrogant certainty, forcing us to work through our faith? Is it because faith resides in the absent, and as with the Hebrew Scriptures—no graven images—the evidence is in the absence, especially the absence of Jesus' body? One possibility here is that the gospel is written for believers so the book is written to sustain believers, not persuade unbelievers; it may be that Mark is presupposing knowledge of the resurrection. Or is it because Mark is turning the world's values upside down? Foolishness is wisdom; the only way of preserving your life is to destroy it. In chapter 8, Jesus says, "For those who want to save their life will lose it; and those who lose their life for my sake, and for the sake of the gospel will save it. For what will it profit them to gain the whole world and forfeit their life?" (8:35–37). Is Mark rubbing our noses in the fact that God chose to be revealed to us as a poor, weak person who is killed? Is he reminding us that God's supposed foolishness and weakness are in fact greater than all human cleverness? Is it possible that Jesus' seeming failure mirrors our own journey of faith: that it is in failure rather than worldly success that we often see and grow into deeper relationship with God?

If the answer to at least some of these questions is yes, then Mark introduces a radical way to believe in Christ. Belief does not reside in a clear and certain position about the past. The truth is in Jesus' statement when he heals Jairus' daughter and says, "Do not fear, only believe" (Mark 5:36). Mark appears to set up a choice: you can be a person of fear or a person of faith. It is as if Mark is saying that a person of fear will seek a false certainty while a person of faith will be willing to live in the bleakness sometimes, in a lack of knowledge at other times. The seeming certainties of life will not save you; rather, to gain your life, you must lose it. The only choice is to learn to live with uncertainty.

The mystics remind us that we will have moments of bleakness and the feeling of spiritual stagnation—and the necessity of walking through them. And these are related to Jesus' own suffering on the cross. That is part of our faith journey, too. Evelyn Underhill wrote to one of her spiritual directees: "After all, if you choose Christ you start on a route that goes over Calvary, and that means the apparent loss of God as a bit of it. . . . Remember it is you who are temporarily blinded, not the world that has gone black."[27]

It is unsettling, and from time to time we will be grateful for the more triumphant and heroic endings to the gospels of Luke and Matthew. But Mark injects an important ingredient into our faith, keeping us right-sized and thus keeping us united as the body of Christ. The Gospel of Mark is an important corrective to the triumphal nature of aspects of Christian faith.

## Salvation and Uncertainty

What, then, of salvation—which has so often been explained in terms of certainty? Isn't it in an assurance of salvation that our faith resides? The great promise of the Christian faith is that through Christ we are saved and guaranteed everlasting life. Otherwise, to return to our opening discussion, we merely return to the dust from whence we have come. That looming reality can create anxiety in even the most devout of Christians. One of the greatest theologians of the twentieth century, Karl Barth, was in old age too afraid to go to sleep at night in case he died in his sleep. It is not my intention to pick on Barth's frailties, but rather to suggest that such fears are far more common among the Christian devout than we usually acknowledge. This raises the question of how we might have a faith that does not give rise to such anxieties.

The logic of some being saved and some being damned has caused exceptional anxiety; it has also given rise to exceptional arrogance in equal measure. Calvin taught the doctrine of predestination (that there were the elect and the reprobate) but always warned his fellow human beings against trying to discern who belonged in which camp; this did not stop his followers guessing and some of them were notoriously self-righteous in their judgments. Nor did it stop them trying to prove they were the elect—ironically—through many good works. This is the special club or "who's in/who's out" mentality which can lead to splitting, division, and exclusion.

In the end, who is saved must necessarily be a mystery and is not for us to judge: to do so would be to take on the role of God. In short, faith is not grounded in certainty about where we will land upon our deaths. Faith is belief in a God whose graciousness and love are quite beyond our comprehension, such that the exact dimensions of the afterlife are quite properly beyond our imagination. This realization, this acceptance of mystery, if you like, prepares us to map a fresh approach to death and to salvation—which is the path of this life.

## Saved by Love

There is a passage in Luke's gospel that may be especially helpful here, in which the Sadducees ask Jesus a trick question (Luke 20:27–40). The Sadducees formed the most conservative party in first-century Judaism. They believed only in the Torah, the first five books of the Hebrew Scriptures (the "Books of Moses") and refused to entertain any doctrine not contained in this narrow canon. They pose this complicated query to Jesus:

> Teacher, Moses wrote for us that if a man's brother dies, having a wife but no children, the man must take the wife and raise up children for his brother. Now there were seven brothers, the first took a wife, and died without children; and the second and the third took her, and likewise all seven left no children and died. Afterwards the woman also died. In the resurrection, therefore, whose wife will the woman be? For the seven had her as a wife?

In asking Jesus this question they were not really concerned about the afterlife; they did not believe in the resurrection of the body because they could not find the doctrine in the Torah (the Pharisees and other Jews in the first century did believe in it, appealing to other scriptural texts). The Sadducees' intention was to ridicule Jesus by asking for a certain answer to a question that was designed not to have one. We all know people like this, ready and wanting to catch us out at any moment.

As he often did in situations like this, Jesus turned the tables on them, and outwitted them on their own scriptural terms. They asked him a question based on the Levirate law of marriage (Deuteronomy 25:5–6, the object of which was to provide a legal heir for a man who died childless). Jesus replied with a text from Exodus 3:6, in which Moses suggests that all human beings, whether dead or alive in human terms, are alive to God. "Now he is not God of the dead, but of the living," Jesus says, "for all live to him." Using their own scriptures, Jesus asserts that the boundary between life and death is a very thin one, important only to human beings. God's love is the only thing that is important, and it penetrates both realities.

If both the dead and the living are alive to God, and our life is a preparation for death, then how shall we live? How shall we approach death? A desire for certainty can lead us down the path of either despair or self-righteousness, and neither really prepares us for death. But faith in the God of love draws us back to a path of preparation: it calls us to the expression of love in all that we do, by which we might reflect the love of God and become most fully who we are called to be. This forces us to look outward, to love neighbor and love God. And it prepares us to look inwards with confidence, to see ourselves as received and loved—wholly and completely—by the God who created us. Confident in this, we may meet death or, as Job puts it, then we shall behold God, and not another.

Dust may be that most democratic of substances, and for some a subsequent cause for anxiety; the faithful rejoinder is that God's saving love is the most democratic of all loves, available to all people, everywhere.

## The Thorny Doctrine of the Atonement

There remains a stumbling block to Christian faith, one that raises fundamental questions about God's love. This is the doctrine of the atonement with which we began the chapter. It is a huge topic, and I can only touch on it here, but we need to weigh what it means in terms of a practical Christianity, for what we think about it may determine our actions towards others and our attitude to God.

Christ has saved us: that is a distinctive expression of the Christian faith. But how does that salvation occur and what is its nature? Earlier in this chapter, I suggested that there is a version of Christian theology that rests on a particular kind of certainty about the death of Jesus as a supreme sacrifice to make amends for the sins of the world. I suggested that certainty of this sort essentially negates the vulnerable cry of Jesus on the cross. It also takes away the experience of being swept up into the life of God with others. In short, life in God is something we experience, not something we have to get right: it is a practice rather than a doctrine.

This is not to negate sin, but it is to declare that God's love is greater than human sin. The vital question here is this: is our starting point human sin or the love of God? The former narrative of the atonement always begins with human sin. But for me, the starting point is always God's unconditional love for us just as we are, with all our failures as well as our hopes. We begin with—and return again and again to—the exploration of faith from the experience of God's love.

To open ourselves to God's expansive and unconditional love is quite alien in our society. We live in a culture of self-help books, self-reliance, and enormous loneliness—both real and existential. We are rarely encouraged to turn to others for help. We rarely feel able to make ourselves that vulnerable. How many of us could really cry out our pain, the way the Psalmists do, without fear of being rejected for it? Most of us feel that we have to cope with, mop up, bear our pain quite by ourselves, hide away the things that are apparently bad about ourselves, all the time conforming ourselves to a particular self we think we ought to be.

The film *American Beauty* (released in 1999) revolves around "the most unhappy marriage in American suburbia," as I remember one reviewer putting it, in which husband (Kevin Spacey) and wife (Annette Bening) try to sort out their problems utterly isolated from each other or any real friends. In one scene the character played by Bening, a real estate agent, arrives at a house that she plans to show to prospective buyers that day. It is a dull and depressing house with ugly wallpaper, the epitome of bad suburban architecture, and it has been left in a filthy and grimy state by the owners. She strips off her smart linen dress and jacket, and cleans the entire house in her underwear and high heels, scrubbing kitchen tiles and vacuuming manically, all the while saying as a mantra: "I *will* sell this house today. I *will* sell this house today." At the end of the day, having failed to sell the horrible house, she leans against the window and crumples into tears, only to pull herself up short and slap herself on the cheeks, saying "Pull yourself together." That scene of her edginess, her repressed pain, erupting into uncontrollable tears, repeats several times in the film, and each time she slaps herself back into control. It is symbolic of how, in contemporary American and British (indeed, Western) culture, our isolated and isolating ways of coping with pain and self-loathing fail us. Unfortunately, we do not know where to look for another answer; we think there is no other way.

Self-will, and an abiding belief in our willpower, may be two cardinal sins of our age, for they trick us into believing that we can totally control and cope with every aspect of our lives, our emotions, our pain. They prevent us from *experiencing* faith as the transformation of our lives, and make us think that faith is about getting it right. I am not advocating an abdication of responsibility for our actions—far from it— but I am suggesting that opening ourselves to God's mercy and love, praying for God's help in seemingly impossible circumstances, takes us into a realm beyond that of our own making, into the realm of grace. And we often receive and experience grace in very ordinary ways: the listening ear of a friend; the realization that we have someone who can do the shopping when we are too ill to do it ourselves; asking another for help and discovering their sheer joy at giving it; being vulnerable with a friend and having them respond by sharing something they could never before speak out loud.

We have a choice, then, about where we start the salvation narrative. If we begin with certainty and sin, everything has to operate around those forces. God is then an angry and judgmental deity who planned for his own son to die in order to "do something" about sin and fix the broken contract with humankind. In this version, Jesus is the scapegoat who will take away sin for the rest of us—as long as we accept this formulation. Inevitably, this theory of the atonement sets up a group of the good and saved ones—on the inside—and the rest, those bad ones on the outside who have not accepted this story or its consequences.

The problem with this version—and many do find it deeply troubling—is that it is always a story of insiders and outsiders. There always has to be some wicked other on the outside in order to explain the continuance of sin. The rejection and scapegoating of Jesus on the cross is replayed again and again, as others who will not conform to a particular theory, a particular group mentality, are likewise scapegoated. There are endless examples of this tragic pattern in history. Think of the scapegoating of the Jews in 1930s Germany; they were blamed for the country's economic misfortunes, in just the way that they have frequently been blamed for the death of Jesus, with horrendous consequences. Thus, disunity is at the heart of things from the very beginning. Following this theological perspective, we can never hope to be the body of Christ except in making—whether in reality or in our imaginations—a group of bad guys against which to measure our goodness.

But if the love of God is the starting point, then God is at the very center and we as human beings are God's creatures, always already loved by God. Now we can set out on the open-ended adventure of a Christian life. Faith becomes not the attempt to conform to a particular theory or doctrine, a particular morality, a particular group mentality, a particular scheme, but rather an adventure in which we are constantly surprised by grace, and open to that surprise. Think of the disciples on the Emmaus road. The last thing they expected was to have a chat, to eat a meal, with the risen Lord. It is on the journey that we grow in relationship with Jesus and find ourselves redeemed.

## Drawing Near the Cross

You might well be asking: where is the crucified Christ in this, if not part of God's scheme to repair the covenant with a disobedient people? Willingly sacrificial, I think, and sharing our pains. His death on the cross is not to appease

God's wrath but is the end point of a life consciously lived in love and for love. As Verna Dozier reminds us:

> I always say Jesus did not get crucified for singing and praying—or even for doing good works. Jesus was crucified for challenging the powers that be, for offering human beings a new possibility for life. He didn't get into trouble for healing the sick, but for healing the sick on the Sabbath. He didn't get into trouble for being pious, but for challenging piety.[28]

Jesus crossed lines and broke rules for the sake of God's love, and he willingly suffered the consequences. The cry, "My God, my God, why hast thou forsaken me?" is the pained cry of a lonely man with natural, human doubts. Mark's gospel strips away the triumph of certainty, and leaves us with a savior who sought the love of God from where he was, just as he was.

Again, we come back to the *experience* of faith; in this case, the experience of Christ who suffers with us and knows our pain. When people wrestle with God, with their faith, they often express that wrestling, that questioning, that uncertainty, in intellectual terms. Take the problem of evil for example. How can a good God allow bad things to happen? That is the popular way of expressing it. Philosophers of religion usually discuss it in the driest language. But the question is not an abstract one. At the heart of that question there always lie real sadnesses and griefs: a child dying; a woman battered by her husband; the death of a loved one in violent circumstances. When faced with those horrors, we do indeed wrestle with God. We are uncertain. We cry out: how can this be?

In the Christian story it is the redeeming work of the incarnate God, Jesus Christ, who answers that cry. The central Christian narrative is that of a man, who was also God, who suffered the very worst of what humans can suffer and do to another human being on this earth, even unto death. This story—at the heart of our faith—teaches us that God is not aloof, for God has borne our pains and knows them. In that sense, to wrestle with God and with our faith, to walk through the uncertainties, is an act of faith, precisely because we are wrestling and walking with a God who comes close enough to identify with our pains and horrors.

## Practicing Uncertainty

How might this alternative framing of salvation affect our *practice* of Christianity? It suggests that the life of faith is an open-ended adventure with a God who loves us and desires our transformation—not into something or somebody that we are not, but, with Christ accompanying us, into the holy people God calls us to be.

That is the nature of salvation: the constant process of being transformed that we might enjoy the fullness of life and enact God's will by taking our part in transforming God's world. It frees us from a need to create groups of those who are in and out, good and bad. It frees us from the need for a bitter-edged certainty, that hard place that the poet Yehuda Amichai wrote about, from which there will be no growth. Far from endangering the world, he says,

> doubts and loves
> dig up the world
> like a mole, a plow.

And a whisper will be heard in the place
where the ruined
house once stood.

We might pray, in response: Gracious God, save us from the hardness of heart that blocks our knowledge of you. Open our eyes to the fullness of this world, and our hearts to the abundance of your love. Amen.

## For Reflection

1. Where do you see the dangers of certainty in your own life and faith? Which of your certainties has begun to feel rigid and counter-productive?

2. For millennia, Christians have understood Jesus' death as a sacrifice to appease God, and assumed that some will be within the saving power of his death and others will be outside. Where have you seen this theology expressed? What are its implications for your own faith and that of the community where you see it lived out?

3. In the film *American Beauty*, the protagonists are isolated and incapable of relying on other people for support, even when they are falling apart. When have you experienced this challenge to need others, and attempted to "pull yourself together" rather than reveal your struggle to others?

4. In his poem "The Place Where We Are Right," Yehuda Amichai presents the hope that we can draw near to God and each other via our pain, failure, and doubts. Recall a time that you experienced failure but found yourself closer to God and others.

*After this, I looked, and lo, in heaven an open door! And the first voice, which I had heard speaking to me like a trumpet, said, "Come up hither, and I will show you what must take place after this." At once I was in the spirit, and lo, a throne stood in heaven, with one seated on the throne! And he who sat there appeared like jasper and carnelian, and round the throne was a rainbow that looked like an emerald. Round the throne were twenty-four thrones, and seated on the thrones were twenty-four elders, clad in white garments, with golden crowns upon their heads. From the throne issue flashes of lightning, and voices and peals of thunder, and before the throne burn seven torches of fire, which are the seven spirits of God; and before the throne there is as it were a sea of glass, like crystal.*

*And round the throne, and on each side of the throne, are four living creatures, full of eyes in front and behind: the first living creature like a lion, the second living creature like an ox, the third living creature with the face of a man, and the fourth living creature like a flying eagle. And the four living creatures, each of them with six wings, are full of eyes all around and within, and day and night without ceasing they sing, "Holy, holy, holy, is the Lord God almighty, who was and is and is to come!"*

*And whenever the living creatures give honor and glory and thanks to him who is seated on the throne, who lives forever and ever, they cast their crowns before the throne, singing, "Worthy are you, our Lord and God, to receive glory and honor and power; for you did create all things, and by your will they existed and were created."*

*Revelation 4 (RSV)*

## Glimpsing God

We sense God, most often, by "traces": traces of the transcendent within the earthly; traces of the eternal brought into the finite world of our lives. The American poet Virginia Hamilton Adair captures this sense of entering into the landscape of the sacred in her poem "Entrance."

> We have all known, now and then,
> that the place is always there, waiting,
> ours for the asking,
> for the silent stepping out of ourselves
> into solace and renewal.
> We do not even need a gate,
> though it can be pleasantly awesome,
> a ritual of entrance.
> Some walk straight in,
> through the invisible wall of wonder.
> Some scramble through a hedge of thorns,
> thankful for the pain, the bright drops of blood.
> Some enter over the token length of wall;
> They like the solid scrape of stone,
> the breathless act of climbing.
> Once we are in, no matter how,
> the secret terrain goes on forever.
> When we forget it is there,
> then it is gone,
> and we are left outside
> until we remember.[29]

We all know those moments when we catch a sense of the mystery beyond us: in breathless exhilaration from the top of a mountain, in seeing a piece of art that so captures our imagination that we see something ordinary in an extraordinary way, in walking into the garden in the early morning and finding the brilliance of color in flowers that have just opened, or in eating something utterly delicious. We sense the divine presence in the beauty of creation and in those things that we create when we are at our best as human beings. We have all been in beautiful buildings that have inspired our awe—great cathedrals, intimate chapels— or we have heard a piece of music that has moved us beyond ourselves.

This glimpsing of the eternal and transcendent often happens randomly and spontaneously, and that is a gift. I always remember my sister and brother-in-law describing how, on an evening stroll in France, they walked into the Sainte-Foy abbey-church in Conques in France and heard one of the monks playing the organ. The evening turned to dusk; the church became completely dark, and glorious music filled the space, giving them—both generally agnostic in their attitude to religion—what they described as a sense of God's presence. When they stepped out into the street, they realized that there had been dozens of other passers-by in the church too, hidden in the darkness but drawn by the glorious music into a mysterious communion with one another and with God.

Experiences like these are at the heart of John's vision in Revelation, when he announces, "I looked, and lo, in heaven an open door! . . . At once I was in the spirit, and lo, a throne stood in heaven, with one seated on the throne!" (Revelation 4:1–2, RSV). John goes on to describe in careful detail a God who is quite beyond human imagination. Certainly, God is at the center of the scene. And yet it is not the figure of God that is described: there is merely the passing reference to God being like jasper and carnelian, the brilliance of precious stones; but that tells us very little about God. At most, he borrows from the first chapter of Ezekiel in his vision, where "something that seemed like a human form" is seated on a throne, amidst winged creatures, lightning and wheels and fire. This is, says Ezekiel, "the appearance of the likeness of the glory of the Lord" (Ezekiel 1:26, 28).

William Blake, *Four and Twenty Elders* (1805)
Credit: Tate, London / Art Resource, NY

Though John could not find words to describe God, some artists have tried to capture John's vision on canvas with the ironic conclusion that they end up trying to depict God. William Blake's watercolor *Four and Twenty Elders*, painted in 1805 and now in the Tate Gallery in London, combines the elements of Revelation 4 (and, in turn Ezekiel 1) to produce a depiction of splendor and majesty: rainbow, bowing figures, the swirl of eyes and the evocation of Ezekiel's wheels. But the enthroned divinity at the center of the painting takes us back to the anthropomorphic God who is, once again, an old man with a beard.[30]

A less well-known depiction of Revelation 4 is that by the Australian twentieth-century artist Grace Cossington Smith, painted in 1952–53. Cossington Smith painted it after a visit to Europe, and the great Renaissance depictions of religious subjects echo in the almost mosaic-like quality of the painting and in its style: it's a bit like a fresco in a medieval church. Cossington Smith's God is another man with a beard, and many of the twenty-four elders seem to be tipping their bottoms into the air, giving (unintentionally, I suspect) a comical air to the scene.

In neither Blake's nor Cossington Smith's paintings does the depiction of "God" work. How could it? For all their greatness as painters, neither Blake nor Cossington Smith succeeds because the task is beyond any artist: the figure of God has to be painted and yet cannot be painted. Visual artists have to substitute John's wordlessness with a pictorial image, so each artist must work out his or her own image of God. (Cossington Smith was a devout Anglican Christian all her life, while Blake's faith was of a more radical, prophetic, and nonconformist stripe, rather at odds with his depiction of God on a throne.) In doing so they invoke

*A Practical Christianity: Meditations for the Season of Lent*

not the glory of God, but a sense of bathos, something ordinary, even disappointing. But that's inevitable.[31]

Grace Cossington Smith,
*I looked, and behold, a door was opened in Heaven* (1953)
oil on composition board, 86.4 x 59.2 cm
Credit: National Gallery of Australia, Canberra. Used by permission.

Maybe the title of Cossington Smith's painting gives us a clue as to how we should look at it and think about it. Just as the poet Virginia Hamilton Adair borrowed from Revelation 4 the image of an entrance, a gateway or door into a life lived in God's presence, so Cossington Smith's title for her painting is that first line of Revelation 4: *I looked, and behold, a door was opened in Heaven.* In fact, nearly half of the painting is taken up by the door and the observer, the "I" who sees the door and grasps the opportunity to look through it. Perhaps what Cossington Smith's painting does successfully convey is the human experience of "observing" God—always partially, in a glimpse or a glance.

## *Seeking the Unseen God*

The spontaneous glimpse of the divine working in the world is always an unexpected delight, but it can be frustratingly fleeting if we are not intentional about seeking it. As Virginia Hamilton Adair puts it in her poem:

> When we forget it is there,
> then it is gone,
> and we are left outside
> until we remember.

Especially during the season of Lent, with the energy of intention all around, how do we develop a way of life that enables us to be intentional about seeing the world as it is, shot through with God? How do we train ourselves to 'see' in a regular way the God of mystery, the unfathomable, the unseeable, the Creator God? For just about everything in our busy western lives conspires to make us forget. And this is not only in secular culture. The Protestant work ethic beats fast in all our hearts without our even knowing. Try preaching a sermon on the importance of observing the Sabbath to a congregation of workaholic pastors: I have, and was accused of chastising them.

So, on the one side, we have the busyness of everyday life: of working days which extend into evenings, of family life where one meal a week together is a miracle, of working parents for whom multi-tasking is a way of life, of single parents struggling to raise children on the poverty line. On the other side, we have the daunting vastness of the mystery of God, the seeming impossibility of beginning a spiritual life. Is it not easier to rely on those spontaneous glimpses of the divine? Should we not leave consistent praying to those who are called to it—monks and nuns? And yet I think that most people want more. I side with William James who believed that human nature is fundamentally religious.[32] When I pray I long for more, and I know the answer to that is a regular and disciplined prayer life. W. R. Inge, an Anglican priest and theologian who led the revival of interest in mysticism in the early twentieth century, and was for many years Dean of St. Paul's Cathedral in London, wrote, "How can we see God if we do not long to see him? . . . Religion is the thirst for God, and its satisfaction."[33]

So where do we begin? How do we tend to our thirst for God, train ourselves to catch more than random glimpses of God?

# 1. Seeing and Seeking
# God in Spiritual Practice

In 2005, during a sabbatical in Australia, I got appendicitis. Recovering from surgery slowed me down, enabled me to read a great deal and pray more. I read a lot about Australian art in that time. During that visit, I had a conversation with the Australian artist John Olsen, who talked to me about painting the vastness of the Australian landscape, and much of his life's work has been dedicated to that task. How does one begin to paint the great deserts of that country, the land which goes on and on and on, quite unlike anything I have encountered in the small, domestic landscapes of England or even in the vastness of parts of the USA? Olsen's answer is that all the artist can do is look and start to put color on canvas. Olsen is one of Australia's greatest twentieth-century painters, so when he puts color onto canvas, there is not only the skill but also the eye of the supremely accomplished artist at work.

The painting, *Lake Hindmarsh, the Wimmera* (1970), also on the cover of this book, is an example of his work, with one tiny bird winging its way across the desert. The lake only fills from time to time, and in summer it is dry and dusty in parts. Of this painting, Olsen said, "The reason the bird is tiny is that you are tiny in the overwhelming sense of nature and life." We are looking down onto and yet we are also in the landscape. Olsen said at the time he was painting these works, "I am the landscape and the landscape is in me." I found these statements and Olsen's description of how he approaches the mystery of the land, the vastness of the landscape he wishes to bring to the viewer, helpful in thinking about how we approach a spiritual life, especially if we are just beginning or have been out of the habit of regular prayer for a while and want to get back to it.[34]

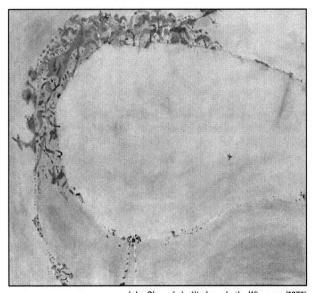

John Olsen, *Lake Hindmarsh, the Wimmera* (1970)

Cultivating a spiritual practice is always available to us. Virginia Hamilton Adair's poem reminds us of that:

> We have all known, now and then,
> that the place is always there, waiting,
> ours for the asking,
> for the silent stepping out of ourselves
> into solace and renewal.

But often the question is: how? Like the Australian desert, the landscape of the spiritual life sometimes seems too huge or too daunting or too bewildering for us to enter. We are the tiny birds. Or maybe we enter it for a bit—we realize we are the spiritual landscape and it is us—and then retreat until we remember it again.

Cultivating a spiritual practice takes time, but it is available to anyone. As John Olsen puts it, all you can do is begin to put color on the canvas. You start somewhere. The spiritual equivalent of putting color on canvas might be saying the Lord's Prayer every time you get into the shower or bath. It might be remembering at certain times of the day or night to give thanks for the beauty of creation. It is the regularity of this engagement that begins to give shape to a prayer life, just as regular exercise gives our bodies definition and keeps us physically fit.

A spiritual practice is not something we do on our own. By taking even five minutes in a day to pray, we are engaging in a relationship with a God who not only created us but also loves us, and therefore wants to be in a relationship with us. Something begins to happen when we engage with that loving God. We are helped in the discipline of prayer; we begin to want that relationship to grow. Five minutes may become ten, even fifteen. And gradually, we realize that through this discipline comes freedom: the freedom of a new relationship that begins to make sense of the rest of our busy lives.

And such a spiritual practice begins to take us into a relationship with a different facet of God. Or, as the mystics would put it, we begin to enter into union with God. It takes us beyond the entrance of the door; we discover that God is not just "out there"—the great unfathomable but glorious creator God—God is with us. God is wherever we are. Evelyn Underhill went so far as to say, "Now it seems to me that one's life only attains in so far as it is consciously lived in the Presence of God. This consciousness can be attained and clung to by a definite act of the will—or rather by a series of graduated acts."[35]

In Cossington Smith's painting of Revelation 4, the observer is always on the outside looking in; God is "out" there, through the door. Notice the set of the observer's head; he is looking up with awe and even a little tentativeness. There is no way that he is going to step across the boundary. But for the poet Adair, entrance through that door is always possible.

> Some walk straight in, through the invisible
>     wall of wonder.
> Some scramble through a hedge of thorns,
> thankful for the pain, the bright drops of blood.
> Some enter over the token length of wall;
> They like the solid scrape of stone,
> the breathless act of climbing.
> Once we are in, no matter how,
> the secret terrain goes on forever.
> We get in by different routes, but we get in.

Grace Cossington Smith, *Open Door* (1960)
Used by permission.

If her paintings are anything to go by, I think Grace Cossington Smith may have known this more intimate side of the spiritual life. Immediately after she painted *I looked, and behold, a door was opened in Heaven*, she began to paint a whole series of interiors, for which she became particularly famous, such as *Open Door* (1960). These are calm, homely spaces, full of bright colors, with traces of their occupants strewn across beds, chairs, and sewing tables. Cossington Smith was certainly interested in making the invisible visible—she had tried it with the painting of Revelation 4. Now she was making her quiet, rather homely life visible and, moreover, its spiritual joys visible. As Druscilla Modjeska puts it in her book about Cossington Smith, "It's as if she pushed open that door, stepped through, and found that the vision of heaven was where she was all the time—in her own bedroom."[36] The result is these extraordinary light-filled, colorful interiors; truly luminous and radiant.

## 2. Seeking and Seeing
## God in Our Worship

It is in our worshipping life that we may train ourselves to "see" in a regular way the God of mystery, the unfathomable, the un-seeable Creator God.

As we have seen, John's vision in Revelation avoids describing *God*—the central figure who sits on the throne. Rather, what is described is the scene surrounding God: a rainbow and twenty-four further thrones on which twenty-four elders sit, dressed in white robes with gold crowns on their head. There is thunder and lightning, flaming torches and something like a sea of glass or crystal. It's dramatic. And then there are the four creatures—faces like a lion, ox, human being, and eagle—and they sing night and day of God's glory and greatness and infinity. Their purpose is to praise God, to sing "Holy, holy, holy, the Lord God the almighty, who was and is and is to come." And their song of praise inspires the twenty-four elders to cast their crowns before God's throne, singing:

> You are worthy, our Lord and our God,
> To receive glory and honor and power,
> For you created all things,
> And by your will they existed and were created.

God is quite beyond the human imagination. This does not mean that we do not, or cannot, know God. Rather, while we "see" God in glimpses, we also "see" God through our worship, as do others, the onlookers. John, the author of Revelation, understood this. And he borrowed from the first chapter of Ezekiel in his vision, where "something that seemed like a human form" is seated on a throne, amidst winged creatures, lightning, and wheels and fire. This is, says Ezekiel, "the appearance of the likeness of the glory of the Lord." It is fascinating that, in a book teeming with colorful and distinct images, many of them used by different factions within Christianity over the centuries to predict this or that about the fate of the world, the image we have of God in that very same book is, in the end, one of glorious mystery. This sense of the ineffability of the divine is echoed in the work of the apophatic theologians we discussed in the last chapter.

We use our God-given gifts to sing, "Holy, holy, holy, the Lord God the almighty, who was and is and is to come"—and indeed we still sing this in worship, as the church has done throughout the ages—and in the very act of singing God's praises we begin to perceive the nature of God. As Evelyn

Underhill writes: "Worship, in all its grades and kinds, is the response of the creature to the Eternal."[37]

It is in disciplined and regular worship that we are welcomed to perceive God, for it is in glorifying God that we sense God's glory. It is in participating that we receive. And even if we stray off for a bit, even when we think we cannot fathom God or ask why we would believe in God, even when we make it all very complicated in our minds, God's glory is always there, ready to be appreciated and glimpsed whenever we turn our hearts and minds and sensibilities towards that which is beyond us and yet entirely a part of our daily lives. For, like the creatures and the elders in the Book of Revelation, one of the tasks of the faithful is to worship God regularly and corporately so that onlookers will perceive the existence and nature of the holy, precisely because of what we are doing. Our prayer life therefore becomes a witness to the very existence and nature of God. And while individual prayer is essential, so is public corporate worship, not least as a testimony to our faith. God is "seen" not only by us but also by others, through our worship.

## The God Who Is Incarnate

When we emphasize the mystery of God—and there is great importance in doing that, for it is part of that uncertainty that is essential for faith, and that enables us to remain right-sized about what we know about God—there is nevertheless the danger that we eclipse the unique and extraordinary story that is at the heart of the Christian faith. This is the story of the incarnate God, the second person of the Trinity, in which God catapulted himself into the world to share the mess and troubles of human lives. The infinite became finite; the God of mystery came down from the "throne that is a rainbow that looks like an emerald" (as John puts it in Revelation) and took on the body and life of a Jewish man.

Evelyn Underhill was aware of this danger of over-emphasizing the mystery of God, and was urged by her own spiritual director, Baron Von Hugel, to cultivate more intentionally a devotion to Christ in her prayer life. She wrote, even before she met Von Hugel: "Everyone tends to worship God more under one aspect than another. The Trinity is far too great to be apprehended 'evenly all around' by any one consciousness. Tyrell said that everyone was either a God-lover or a Christ-lover; and no one was both, at any rate in an equal degree." And she wrote to her own spiritual directee: "Why was God revealed in Christ, except that such a revelation was an absolute necessity for the majority of human souls?"[38]

Let's look at a well-known story in the gospels. It takes place in the home of two women—the first-century equivalent of Grace Cossington Smith's interiors in the suburbs of Sydney, which she shared with her sister Madge—to think further about the intimacy of a relationship with the Incarnate God. This is the story of Mary and Martha in the Gospel of Luke (10:38-42).

> Now as they went on their way, he [Jesus] entered a certain village, where a woman named Martha welcomed him into their home. She had a sister named Mary, who sat at the Lord's feet and listened to what he was saying. But Martha was distracted by her many tasks; so she came to him and asked, "Lord, do you not care that my sister has left me to do all the work by myself?

Tell her then to help me." But the Lord answered her, "Martha, Martha, you are worried and distracted by many things; there is need of only one thing. Mary has chosen the better part, which will not be taken away from her."

This is a familiar story, interpreted in numerous ways over the centuries. Sometimes it is seen as representing the split between the contemplative life and the apostolic life, with the contemplative (Mary) as the winner. Sometimes it is held up as an example of the feminist Jesus who welcomes women into the inner circle of disciples. Other readers of the text see the story as an instance of Jesus' ability to negotiate very neatly a family quarrel: clearly Martha is angry at Mary for not doing enough work in the kitchen and tries to win Jesus over to her side in what may be a long-running battle between the two sisters. Her strategy backfires, as Jesus gently makes the point that hospitality is, quite simply, about paying attention to the guest, and in return, the giver of hospitality (the listener) will receive. Yet others have pointed to the human-ness or believability of the characters in Luke's story: we can identify with Jesus' position in Mary and Martha's home because we all know how uncomfortable it is to visit friends and be caught in a family argument, or to feel embarrassed because our host is fussing too much over the tiniest details when a simple meal or cup of coffee would be quite enough.

All of these interpretations carry weight, but it seems to me that a key point of the story is simply about making space and time to listen to God. For that is what Mary does. She sits at Jesus' feet and listens to him speak; she listens to Jesus' words (*logos* is the Greek used here), and thus to the Word, to God.

Jesus says, "Martha, Martha, you are anxious and troubled by many things. But there is need for only one. Mary chose the good part. It won't be taken away from her." But what is that good thing? Scribes, copying out this gospel before print was invented, often amended this text: thinking it was referring to the number of dishes Martha was preparing, they changed "one" to "a few" and caused considerable confusion. But Luke here seems rather to be referring to the one good thing required of hospitality, and that is to pay attention to the guest. The context is important, for in paying attention to the guest, Mary is paying attention to God. It is not that she could not have done the cooking if required; as Underhill put it, "Appearances notwithstanding, Mary would probably have been a better cook than Martha, had circumstances forced on her this form of activity."[39] But she chose at that moment to pay attention to the guest. If we are too busy to listen to our guest, we will miss the gift they have to give to us. This is why she has chosen the good or better part. There is a moral dimension to this: Mary made the right choice.

In making moral choices about our lives and the world, in trying to live a holy life, we often make ourselves very busy. Busyness is needed, for justice, for joining with God in building the kingdom of heaven on earth. And this is right: spirituality and justice are not separate categories. When we consider the way to follow Jesus, we tend to think first about feeding the poor, healing the sick, loving our neighbor. But do we give ourselves enough time in all of that busyness to listen to God, to see and perceive and drink in the glory of God? Do we "tune in" to God? Do we remember, in our discipleship, to follow the Jesus who went into the desert to pray for forty days, who took himself up mountains and deliberately went away from the crowds at certain points in his public ministry so that he could spend time in prayer and contemplation? The gospel suggests that there is a moral component to Mary's listening. It is right to give time to a guest. It is right to listen. It is right to listen to God, who is always present if we open ourselves up, to give ourselves time to be mindful of the holy, to be alert to the sacred. It is right because if we do not pay attention in all our busyness, for all our conviction that we are living the gospel and being good Christians, we will wake up one day to find that we are ignoring the central figure—God.

At the core of the worshipping life of a Christian is the Eucharist, which reminds us always of the life and death of Jesus Christ. Although the passage from Revelation 4 puts God the Creator, the God of mystery, at the center of the ceaseless worshipping scene, once we read on to chapter 5, it is revealed that the Lamb, representing Christ, is there too, between the throne and the four living creatures, and amongst the twenty-four elders, "standing as if it had been slaughtered." As the observer watches the scene, so the four living creatures and the twenty-four elders move towards the Lamb and bow down before him. Their song is now changed: "Worthy is the Lamb that was slaughtered to receive power and wealth and wisdom and might and honor and glory and blessing!" (Revelation 5:12). The four living creatures declare "Amen," and the twenty-four elders now fall down and worship the lamb. The objects of worship in this extraordinary, majestic scene are therefore both transcendent and redemptive. Here is the Eternal God, "the Lord God almighty, who was and is and is to come," and yet here also is the Incarnate God, Jesus Christ, who died on the cross. And while the God of mystery, the Creator God, is never described, the Lamb is in plain sight for all to see.

Every time we celebrate the Eucharist, we Christians believe that God is in plain sight—there on the altar in the bread and wine, the body and blood of Christ. When we reach out our hands for the bread and wine, we do not just see God, but we also touch and eat God. This is the living presence of God. And in reaching out for that bread and wine and eating it, over and over again we make and re-make the body of Christ—joining with all other Christians, regardless of the differences between us, to know each other and be known in our response to God. As David Stancliffe puts it, "As we receive the broken fragment of the consecrated bread into our hands, we are offered transformation: a change from being the broken, discordant and fragmentary people that we are into being renewed and whole, members of one single body, ready to act as one."[40] We become what we receive and perceive: the body of Christ.

## The God Who Is Change

What are we to say of the third person of the Trinity? How do we grow our capacity to "see" the Holy Spirit?

We can begin to discern the presence of the third person of the Godhead, as we see the lives of those around us, and our own lives, being transformed by God. There is undoubtedly a moral and indeed prophetic dimension to a life of prayer: we pray "thy kingdom come" in the faith that it *will* —because, slowly, slowly, we will become conformed in the image and likeness of Christ. Every day we are faced with moral choices about how to bring that about. Those moral choices require discernment. Life is messy and we have to figure out how to deal with it. Here's a hunch: it is when we have the balance right between the glory of the mysterious, ultimately un-describable creator God and the intimacy of the incarnate God that we can begin to make those moral choices, in part because we can begin to discern the presence of the third person of the Godhead, the Holy Spirit, acting in our lives, the lives of those around us, and the world at large. Too much of the unfathomable God on a throne—and God becomes too distant, always on the other side of the door; then we have no ability to understand how that very same God may be at work in the world today. Too much of the intimacy of Jesus the man—and we become too sure that we know God's will for us, especially when we rely solely on a few carefully selected scriptural texts which underscore our prejudices but enable us to say that something is "biblical"; then we run the risk of ignoring the action of the Holy Spirit in the lives of others, running roughshod over their experiences of God. Faith is partly about accepting the paradox that God is always both ultimately unknowable and intimately known. And we need this "both/and" in order to discern the movement of the Holy Spirit in our lives today.

Again, worship serves as a locus for the Spirit's revelation. We participate in the corporate worship of the church, putting aside differences and joining with others to become the body of Christ and to worship God together. Evelyn Underhill reminds us that "the Church is not a collection of prize specimens, but a flock" and worship is "an opportunity for the whole Body, sinking differences of understanding and feeling, to join Angels and Archangels, saints and elders, and all the creatures of the earth and sea in praising and glorifying the Holy Name."[41] In worshipping God, we are caught up in the great chain of Christians who have responded to the gospel message, and thus we open ourselves up to change, to the transformation that is at the heart of faith. David Stancliffe puts it like this in his book *God's Pattern*:

> The heart of the faith is about change, the change that God longs to see in us and in everyone. . . . And we don't walk alone; people have trodden before us and blazed the trail—that's the role of the saints—and we catch our hand into the hand of the person in front and get swept up into this great conga or chain.[42]

We yearn for transformation, but we do not make it happen: God does, by the power of the Holy Spirit. Our job is to be fully present and receptive, so that the Holy Spirit can work in our lives. Participation in this mystery is an assent to opening ourselves up to being transformed, to committing ourselves as disciples in the transformation of the world.

People find it notoriously difficult to think about the Trinitarian nature of God. And there were a lot of very technical theological debates about the precise nature of the persons of the Godhead in the fourth and fifth centuries. But one way into the Trinity is to look at how the Holy Spirit gives us a glimpse into the nature of God. If the Christian life is about change, and I think it is, then the ever-present person of the Godhead, the Holy Spirit, is the agent of change in our lives. The Spirit is the unrepentant disturber: the one who urges us into the transformation of ourselves and the world, the ongoing presence of God cheering us on. The Baptist theologian Paul Fiddes made me think more radically about this. When I discussed this with him, he agreed with me in thinking of the Spirit in this way. In fact, he said that he always thinks of the Spirit as the joker in the pack, that part of the Trinitarian God that calls *us* to change. But, he suggested, it is also that part of the Trinitarian God that is always calling *God* to change. The Spirit is often thought of as that part of the Trinity that binds the relationship of the Father and the Son together. But what if it is also that part of the Trinity that constantly opens up that relationship and thus opens up the Creator God's relationship to his Creation? What if the Spirit is the unrepentant disturber of God within Godself?[43]

If this is the case, then the Trinitarian God's calls for us to change are not merely calls to obedience to an unchanging God, calls to respond according to some master plan for change. Rather, they are the calls of a co-Creator who works with us in the unfolding of history. In this sense, God is always bringing us to a renewed vision of God's purpose in the world, but God too is always renewing God's own vision of the world. God is always encouraging us to take risks as God's people in our journey towards fulfillment in Christ, but God too is always taking risks in God's own relationship with Christ and thus in God's relationships with us. The greatest risk was in becoming incarnate in the person of Jesus of Nazareth.

## Seeing the Trinity

We "see" God by making time for the God of mystery who is out of time, for the incarnate God who came into time, for the ever-present Holy Spirit who is in time. We take time to look for the traces of God and God's glory. We enter into a relationship with God who is unknown and known and ever present because we thirst for that relationship. And we welcome and know God as we welcome change into our lives. As W. R. Inge wrote,

> You have not yet lost the wholesome appetite which makes the soul cry, "My soul is athirst for God; when shall I come to appear before the presence of God?" Recollect; think; pray; do not always be in such a hurry. You know well, when you do stop to think seriously, that you are not satisfied. There is something wanting. You have been thirsty without knowing it. Well, that thirst is the craving which God has put into you, because He wishes to satisfy it with himself. Blessed are they that thirst. . . . "Ye are as holy as ye truly wish to be holy," said one of the old mystics.[44]

## For Reflection

1. When have you most clearly "seen" God?

2. What do you do in order to cultivate your own spiritual life?

3. Evelyn Underhill observed that "Everyone tends to worship God more under one aspect than another. The Trinity is far too great to be apprehended 'evenly all around' by any one consciousness." With which person of the Trinity do you most strongly connect?

4. The author asserts that "Christian life is about change" and that the Holy Spirit is the agent of that change. Do you agree?

# CHAPTER 5

# Love

The Pharisees asked Jesus, "Teacher, which is the great commandment in the law?" and he said to them, "'You shall love the Lord your God with all your heart, and with all your soul, and with all your mind.' This is the great and first commandment. And the second is like it, 'You shall love your neighbor as yourself.' On these two commandments depend all the law and the prophets."

*Matthew 22:36–40*

# The Church and the World

At the end of the Eucharist, we are sent out "to love and serve the world." The concluding prayer for Episcopalians says: "And now, Father, send us out, to do the work you have given us to do, to love and serve you, as faithful witnesses of Christ our Lord." In *Common Worship*, the authorized prayer book of the Church of England, we find the prayer: "Almighty God, we thank you for feeding us with the body and blood of your son Jesus Christ. Through him we offer you our souls and bodies to be a living sacrifice. Send us out in the power of your Spirit to live and work to your praise and glory."[45] We are sent out to put into practice what we have become: Christ's body on earth. Ours are the only hands and feet that Christ has now, as the sixteenth-century mystic and Carmelite reformer Teresa of Avila said.

When we are sent out into the world at the end of the Eucharist, when we heed God's command to love our neighbors as ourselves, we need to ask what that *means*. In order to ask that, we need to think about the relationship between the church and the world. Christianity has always had a paradoxical attitude to the world, and the doctrine of the incarnation bears it out. On the one hand, God so loved the world that God sent the only begotten one, who healed the sick, fed the poor, raised the dead, and lived, preached, ate, and made friends in the world alongside ordinary human beings, who joined him in healing the sick, feeding the hungry, and raising the dead. On the other hand, those actions of Jesus of Nazareth meant that he eventually came into conflict with the world, as he challenged human priorities and institutions; this was a conflict that led ultimately to the cross.

Bearing that paradox in mind, I want to sketch four

possible models of the relationship between the church and the world.

*Model 1:* Christians assume the world is a very bad and corrupting place, and choose to stay away from it, building separate, gathered, sometimes utopian communities. An example of this would be the Amish people: descendants of the sixteenth-century Anabaptists who rejected the relationship between church and state that reformers like Luther and Calvin maintained. Some of the earliest Christians would fit this model, too, including the author of the epistle to Diognetus, who wrote in the middle of the second century that Christians "live in their own countries, but only as resident aliens."[46] Today the theology and ethics of Christian thinkers such as the Mennonite John Howard Yoder or Stanley Hauerwas continue to support this model, albeit not in this extreme form.

*Model 2:* Christians assume the world is a very bad place, because it is fallen, but they are committed to making it more godly, chiefly by converting as many people as possible to Christianity. Individual sinners must be saved in order to redeem the world. This model can also be quite practical. Influential evangelicals in Britain and America in the early nineteenth century, for example, worked with these presuppositions about the world, and because of their beliefs, brought such pressure to bear that they toppled the slave trade and then slavery itself.

*Model 3:* Christians still assume the world is a bad place, but there is hope that we can make it better: we can build the kingdom of heaven on earth. Christians do not withdraw from the world, nor do they simply try to grow their own ranks. They must get their hands dirty to change things. They love their neighbors as part of making the world a better place. Many of the nineteenth- and early twentieth-century Social Gospel Christians fit this framework, including Jane Addams, who set up Hull House in Chicago.

*Model 4:* Christians believe the world is essentially mixed, containing some bad but also some good. We remember that God loved the world enough to become incarnate, which also means we do not need to bring Christ to the world, because Christ is already in the world. Those who practice this model must be aware of an inherent tension: by loving as God loved the world, they should expect to come into conflict with the powers that be, as Jesus did.

By instinct and upbringing I know that I fit into the third model, having grown up in a Christian household in which the feeding of the poor and the housing of the homeless was paramount, but I am trying to grow into the fourth model. Let me explain why, beginning first with a story.

## Listening to the World

A year or two after I had been ordained, I went for my ministry review with the Bishop of Oxford, a wise man named Richard Harries. A couple of weeks before such a review, you have to fill out a self-assessment form which has questions about what you think you do best and what you still need to work on, your spiritual life, the things you enjoy about ministry, any problems you are having, and so on. One of the questions is: what do you do to get away from the job? I'm sure you are supposed to give an answer like golf or fishing. Instead I wrote: "Spend time with my atheist friends who are skeptical about the church but support my being a priest." After I had put the form in the mail, I was a bit worried, and thought I should have put something harmless like bird watching. In the interview with the bishop, when we got to that section of the form, his comment was both interesting and helpful. He said: "It's very good that you've got these friends because we must listen to what people are saying outside the church."

I have thought a lot about his words, because this injunction to listen disrupts the ethical paradigm in which Christians have almost always operated in relation to the world, to say nothing of the way we have practiced the command "to love thy neighbor." Listening puts love into a different frame. The emphasis has been on what Christians will do in—or say to—"the world." The question has not so often been framed in terms of what the world gives to us, what we can learn from people outside the church. Take Paul writing to the Thessalonians—"So deeply do we care for you that we are *determined* to share with you not only the gospel of God but also our own selves . . . " (1 Thessalonians 2:8). The pattern is thus: from us to them, never them to us. Even that great commandment to "Love thy neighbor as thyself" is about what we might do to or for another person. It is not about what love, wisdom, support, and kindness we might receive. This can make the relationship between the Christian and "the other" (the worldly one) paternalistic, and therefore not truly mutual or equal.

But if we believe God is already in the world (without our help, thank you very much), that the world is a good place in many ways, that the incarnation is a sign of God's overwhelming love for the world, then we must be willing to receive and listen. We do this not so we can better craft our marketing message to the world. We do it because there is goodness and wisdom and experience in the world, much of which can stand as a necessary corrective to the ways in which the churches have gone wrong, about women and homosexuality and poverty, for example.

An important figure here is William Temple, an Anglican theologian in the first half of the twentieth century in Britain, and ultimately (and briefly) Archbishop of Canterbury. In 1942, in the depths of World War II, Temple's book *Christianity and Social Order* was published. It was reprinted twice in its year of publication and had soon sold over 150,000 copies. It represented Temple's mature thought about the church's relationship to the world, and drew on his pastoral experience, his work as president of the Workers Education Association (an adult education society), his experience of the General Strike in 1926 and the depression of the 1930s, his experience of living in an ailing British Empire, as well as his intellectual analysis of the individual in society. He had, by this time, encountered and learned much from the great American theologian Reinhold Niebuhr. Temple's book was not only popular, it was also influential in laying the foundations for Britain's national health service, which came into existence several years after Temple's death.

Temple believed that there should be no sharp separation between "spiritual" and "material" issues. Putting the doctrine of the incarnation at the center of his theology, he argued that because God came to earth as a human being, there could be no separation between the church and the world. He went on to spell out six principles concerning family life, housing conditions, poverty levels, income and employment, labor, leisure and freedom, that should be every citizen's due. In this, Temple was both visionary and practical.

Furthermore, Temple believed that all human experience was religious or could be interpreted religiously. Christ did not need to be brought into the world—Christ was, is, already in the world. He had learned this particularly from his experience in the sphere of adult education. Far from believing that the church had all the answers, Temple believed that the church must listen to people's personal experiences. In this he foreshadowed the work of the Latin American liberation theologians. He saw personal experience as vital to interpreting the gospel message for and in society: for Temple, you cannot go straight to scripture or doctrine to find easy answers, and then unthinkingly apply them to an ethical or social situation. You have to acquire and assess the evidence, listen to ordinary people's experiences and stories, and harness the work of experts (economists, educators, and so on), to pursue the work of social transformation.

## *The Church Dispersed*[47]

William Temple also stressed the calling of all Christians, lay and ordained, to apply Christian principles in their families, jobs, and civil life. Clergy often forget this. We spend so much of our time preoccupied with the church that we are inclined to forget that the majority of Christians spend most of their week outside the church. We need to shift to a model of the church dispersed rather than the church gathered. In or outside the walls of the church building, we remain the church. And yet I think many of us are taught to compartmentalize our lives, so that we have an acceptable churchy bit and then there is the rest of us, the larger part that is in the world, the part that spends time with spouse or children, family and friends, goes to work, buys the groceries, sleeps, sees movies, reads novels. And yet Jesus longs to be intimately involved in every part of our lives, and to bring love to all of it.

So how do we see what we do in church on a Sunday as fully related to what, as Christians, we do on a daily basis? How do we live out our vocations as Christians as teachers, parents, lawyers, artists, cooks, nurses—in our daily living?

Verna Dozier spoke regularly and compellingly about the vocation and ministry of the laity. She once said, "The layperson's primary function is out there in the world, and it is a problem when the church becomes the primary focus of their lives."[48] Each Christian is called out, to serve and share the love of Christ in the world where we already live and move.

## Christian Witness in a Changing World

The world we are called into is vastly different from the one where William Temple ministered. He was Archbishop of Canterbury at a time when the Church of England still had real status, and the social order was arranged along clear lines of class, gender, and ethnicity. The great post-war immigration patterns had not yet emerged.

The place of religion has shifted immensely in the last sixty years. In England only 6 percent of the population go to church, but more than 50 percent say they believe in God. There is still a state church, but this largely provides a "vicarious religion," as the sociologist Grace Davie puts it, upon which the population can lean in times of crisis—such as the 9/11 terrorist attacks, the major terrorist bombings in London in July 2006, and the death of Princess Diana. Everyone is, by default, a member of the Church of England, unless they actively choose not to be, but that does not mean they give it very much thought or respect.[49]

The decline in churchgoing in Britain is matched in America by the decline in the mainline Protestant denominations. That said, America remains a more religious country than England. If many American visitors to Europe are shocked by its secularity, to the European observer the religiosity of Americans, in at least some parts of the country, is truly astonishing. Over 90 percent of Americans profess belief in God, and only 7.5 percent profess no religion at all. There is a relationship between American identity and religious identity. In this religiosity there is far greater diversity than Britain has ever had. Christian pluralism was there in the modern foundations of this country—Puritan Massachusetts, Quaker Pennsylvania, Anglican Virginia, Baptist Rhode Island, and so on.

But it is not simply a case of unreligious Britain versus religious America. The situation is more complex and nuanced, not least because younger generations are increasingly unchurched, with little or no personal experience or even knowledge of Christianity or the major religions. This is coupled with the rapidity with which communications are changing, and the speed with which younger people integrate these shifts into their lives. Compare this to older generations, who do not always grasp the communications revolution, at least not immediately, but by and large lead churches and manage their messages. The gap is destined only to widen.

Furthermore, both countries are now religiously pluralistic. In the U.S., this has occurred largely as a result of the 1965 New Immigration and Naturalization Act in America, signed by Lyndon B. Johnson at the base of the Statue of Liberty, linked in spirit to the Civil Rights Act of the previous

*A Practical Christianity: Meditations for the Season of Lent*

year. It was intended to end discrimination between peoples and nations. This changed immigration significantly, so that in 1940 Europeans accounted for 70 percent of all immigrants to America; in 1990, this was just 15 percent. Immigrants from the Indian subcontinent and Far East brought their religions with them. This means Buddhism is more diverse in Los Angeles than in any other city in the world, and there are more Muslims in America than there are members of either the Presbyterian or the Episcopal Church.[50] Similarly, after World War II, Britain opened its doors to more immigrants, seeking cheap labor to re-build the country shattered by war, and in 1948 the Nationality Act gave all imperial subjects the right of free entry to Britain. This led to waves of immigration from the Caribbean, parts of Africa, India and Pakistan, Hong Kong, and other parts of the world. We cannot speak of love for our neighbor as ourselves, or explore the relation between church and society, without taking this twenty-first century context into account.

How then do we exercise God's love and demonstrate the knowledge of God's love for all humanity in our present-day contexts? How do we make Christianity viable, plausible, in a skeptical world where so many are convinced that the church is not only ineffectual but also hypocritical? How are we to live as Christians in a religiously pluralistic world? How do those of us who are not fundamentalists present another form of Christianity as viable in the public domain, when the term "Christian" is so often taken to mean conservative or fundamentalist (or both)?

# Loving Our Neighbors Today

I want to take us back to the themes of earlier chapters in the book by way of another illustration. The novelist Catherine Fox writes about the problem I outlined in chapter 3—thinking we have to win God's love by getting everything right—in her novel *Love for the Lost*. Her central character is a young priest, Isobel Knox, who, when the novel opens, is diligent, hard working, ordered in everything she does . . . and irritatingly self-righteous. She rarely takes time off and when she does, it is to do something useful and worthy. Every minute of every day is accounted for. She has not changed much since the days of her school report, which read: "Isobel is helpful and has a keen sense of responsibility. She is always eager to advise other pupils and contribute to class discussion. She is diligent and her work is neat and of a high standard. Her sense of superiority is mellowing and I am sure she will continue to do well when she goes to grammar school in September."

This orderliness, and her attempts to get everything right for God, to win God's love, mean that she is harsh and unforgiving with those who fail—most especially herself. So when suppressed memories of unhappy events in her teenage years begin to resurface, and she falls in love with a married priest and, by way of compensation, has a relationship with a man with whom she is not in love, everything collapses—symbolized by her loss of voice. She is literally unable to speak for several months. She cannot work as a priest, she cannot live alone in her home. She collapses.

So in the end it is Isobel's *failure* that teaches her about God's love. Not her success.

I've worked so hard at serving God and being good, she reflected. Strange to find relief in failure. She'd been like a tightrope artist terrified of falling; but she had fallen, and found that there was a safety-net after all. . . . It was only me that had such exacting standards. Nobody else was expecting me to be perfect. Not God, not Harry [her boss], not the parish.

This puts her in new territory, the territory of God's love. "She was not just a bad servant to be punished. She was a child to be forgiven, and a friend to be helped along by the hand."[51]

God made us, God loves us, and God accepts us as we are. We did not have to earn our creation, and we do not have to earn God's love. But God is delighted when we respond to that love. If we are to bring that love to others, and knowledge of that love to the wider world, then we must know something of what it means to be vulnerable with one another and vulnerable with God. This is what, I think, the fourth model of the church's relationship to the world (the model I find myself striving toward) is about. To learn from others, we have to be vulnerable. If we try to avoid this, we shall revert to a paternalistic "helping" which will have little credibility in our societies today.

We also need to be well informed, just as William Temple insisted. We need to have what the Jesuit lawyer and human rights advocate Frank Brennan calls an "informed conscience." As he puts it, rhetoric about social justice counts for little by way of outcomes unless there is some engagement in the political process and some familiarity with the ways of the law. We need to use the expertise of the world to help us build the kingdom of God on earth, to help us love our neighbors in the most effective way.

I suspect we will also have to do a good deal of listening. This might be frustrating to the activists but it will be essential to anything we do within a multi-cultural and religiously pluralistic society. This will entail listening to each other—especially across religious divides, listening to the Word of God, listening to strangers so that we discover they are not strangers, but all part of the human family. In that way, loving our neighbors as ourselves will begin to become a reality. For we need to know our neighbors to act on God's commandment effectively.

It is very easy to be paternalistic in "helping" those who are on the margins of our societies, to help and direct rather than to listen. One powerful example of the creation of a genuine community that avoids paternalism even as it feeds those who are hungry is the Food Pantry at St. Gregory of Nyssa Episcopal Church in San Francisco. For a start, the food pantry is in the church—not the parish hall or basement—and food is distributed from the sanctuary, around the altar, to about six hundred families every week. Just as striking is the fact that the volunteers who work at the pantry are many of those who came for food and kept coming back—to participate in running it. This is not about "social services to the poor" but the formation of a vital community. The Food Pantry at St. Gregory's has given rise to many more food pantries all over the city of San Francisco and Bay Area, including the Bay View Mission, a joint project of the Diocese of California and Grace Cathedral.

The inspiration for the original St. Gregory's Food Pantry came from Sara Miles, who, twelve years ago, while still a dedicated atheist, walked in off the street and received the bread and wine, the body and blood of Christ—at St. Gregory's everyone is welcome to God's table to receive communion—and had a powerful religious experience that led to her conversion. As she puts it in *Take This Bread*: "Eating Jesus, as I did that day to my great astonishment, led me against all expectations to a faith I'd scorned and work I'd never imagined. The mysterious sacrament turned out to be not a symbolic wafer but actual food—indeed, the bread of life."[52]

Her experience of being fed led her to feed others. She took two engravings on the church's recently installed altar at face value. The first, from the Gospel of Luke, records an insult to Jesus: "This guy welcomes sinners and eats with them." The second, from the seventh-century mystic Isaac of Nineveh, says: "Did not our Lord share his table with tax collectors and harlots? So do not distinguish between worthy and unworthy. All must be equal for you to love and serve."

The food pantry is a eucharistic community, and that also marks it as different. On a Sunday, the congregation sings and dances around the altar; on a Friday, hundreds of people walk around it collecting fresh vegetables, fruit, and basic staples like rice and bread. Liturgy shapes social practice. Here there is no difference between being spiritually fed and literally fed, no difference between the spiritual hunger that leads many to St. Gregory's on a Sunday and the physical hunger of the people who come for their weekly groceries on a Friday.

David Stancliffe writes: "The offering of our lives that we make in worship cannot be satisfied with doing nothing; it calls us to a programme for action to make our world a better place. In other words, to celebrate the Eucharist together and do nothing about feeding the hungry is an act of blasphemy."[53] Ministries like the Food Pantry at St. Gregory of Nyssa model this transformed, mutual, and loving action.

## *The Stranger as Brother and Sister*

Sigmund Freud, in his essay on the uncanny written in 1919, explores the prevalent meanings of the uncanny, which associated it with the unfamiliar, the strange, the *umheim-lich*. And he concludes—through an exploration of dictionary definitions and stories about the uncanny—that the unfamiliar often turns out to be the familiar. The *umheim-lich* is often the *heimlich*. The strange is often the known. Or, to put it in simple Freudian terms, the uncanny can be the return of the repressed.[54]

This is an important insight because it is, of course, easy to be kind to people whom we think of as like ourselves, harder sometimes to show such kindness to strangers. In fact, our current political climate shows how easy it is to fear those we think of as strangers, perceiving them to be outside the fold, unsaved, ungodly; fear all too often turns to hatred, manifested in racism and other forms of prejudice and xeno-phobia. But what Freud teaches us is that the fear or hatred of the supposed other, the supposedly strange, is often the fear or hatred of something within ourselves, our history, our tradition, which we cannot or do not wish to face. The church's anti-Semitism would be an obvious case in point, given our Jewish roots.

In England a few years ago, there was a fascinating series of documentary television programs about the history of slavery in relation to Britain's economy and identity. For example, it traced the ways the slave trade was at the root of much of Britain's wealth in the eighteenth and nineteenth centuries. In one of the programs, two British people went to Jamaica to trace their ancestry: a white woman who discovered that she had black slaves just a few generations back in her family, and a black man who discovered white slave owners in his lineage. Both were surprised and somewhat horrified, the white woman because—coming from rural Kent and having a hobby of collecting English antique cars—she could not believe that she had any "black blood" in her, as she put it; the black man because the presence of a white great-great-grandfather in his family disrupted his black identity, so carefully cultivated in inner-city Birmingham, one of the most racially diverse cities in the UK.

Those whom we might think of as strangers are not so very far from the familiar at all. In being kind to strangers we may discover that we are being kind to our own all long. But that, I think, is the point of the Gospel. The strange remains different, but we engage it because we are to love our neighbors as ourselves. When it comes to showing kindness to strangers, everyone is our brother and sister, just as Jesus relates to his disciples in Matthew's gospel: "Truly I tell you, just as you did it to one of the least of these who are members of my family, you did it to me" (Matthew 25:40).

At the heart of the Christian message is the injunction to embrace our common humanity, to prove by our actions that the stranger is our family. This requires a fierce love, a determined love, in the face of a society that fosters fear and prizes individualism. It requires an openness to God's love which I have described as a spiritual adventure. Mark's gospel, as I suggested, gives us a choice between fear and faith. Love requires faith, even if the outcome is unknown, as it almost always will be.

# From Dust to Glory

I close this chapter and this book knowing this simple truth: that we are surely dust, surely fallen, but that God's love brings us from death to life, or "from dust to glory," as a friend put it after reading through this manuscript.

My friend Anthony Cardovo Campbell was the dean of the chapel at Boston University. A black Baptist who was a canon of an Episcopal Cathedral, a man who had marched with Martin Luther King and gone to Mecca with Malcolm X, he was also an extraordinarily fine preacher. I can still remember (many years later) the sermon he preached when he came to Oxford and to New College Chapel as our guest. It was about bringing dead things to life, based on the story in Luke 6 in which Jesus brings a dead man back to life.

What Anthony emphasized was how exceptionally taboo touching a dead thing was in Jesus's first-century culture. As the dead body was brought on a bier through the streets, people would precede it ringing bells, shouting "dead thing, dead thing" to warn people to flatten themselves against the walls, to get out of the way, to scurry down a side alley, for the dead thing was untouchable. And what did Jesus do? He went straight up to the bier and touched the dead body and brought it to life.

Our task in life, said Anthony, is to touch the "dead things," the untouchables all around us, and bring them to life. This is in part about feeding the hungry and housing the homeless. It is also about welcoming the stranger, the disliked, the untouchable, into the body of Christ. It is even about welcoming the dust-laden parts of ourselves, acknowledging those limits, and asking God to breathe new life into us. For we are all one and the same, made of dust, returning to dust, transformed by God's love.

The words of Mary Oliver remind me of this truth over and over, and never more poignantly than in the poem "In Blackwater Woods."[55] In it, Oliver notices that—in nature as in life—there is a seasonal return to certain tasks and questions, a call to pay attention to those things that are absolutely essential to life.

> To live in this world
> You must be able
> to do three things:
> to love what is mortal;
> to hold it
> against your bones knowing
> your own life depends on it;
> and, when the time comes to let it go,
> to let it go.

Lent is an especially good time to turn back, to practice the art of examination, forgiveness, letting go and consciously turning outward. But the truth is that the process is never completed.

How will we love what is mortal (including ourselves)? How will we learn what we need to let go of, all the time sure that God will never let us go? Such questions take us to the heart of Christian life, which is to say, what it is to be fully alive in this world.

# For Reflection

1. Which of the four models of relationship between the church and the world most closely fits the one you grew up with (if you grew up in a faith community)? Which most closely matches where you are now? Which do you hope to embody?

2. What are some ways you see Christians compartmentalizing our faith? How would you suggest that we relate our activity inside church with our life in the world?

3. The author asks a series of questions on page 89. How would you answer each?

   a. How do we make Christianity viable, plausible, in a skeptical world where so many are convinced that the church is not only ineffectual but also hypocritical?

   b. How are we to live as Christians in a religiously pluralistic world?

   c. How do those of us who are not fundamentalists present another form of Christianity as viable in the public domain, when the term "Christian" is so often taken to mean conservative or fundamentalist (or both)?

4. Whom do you find it most difficult to love? To whom do you find it hardest to listen? How could you more deeply and lovingly engage this "stranger"?

# Notes

1 *Apostolic Tradition* (attributed to Hippolytus of Rome), section 20.

2 On Pachomius, see Philip Rousseau, *Pachomius: The Making of a Community in Fourth-Century Egypt* (Berkeley and Los Angeles: University of California Press, 1999).

3 See Robert Louis Wilken, *The Spirit of Early Christian Thought: Seeking the Face of God* (New Haven and London: Yale University Press, 2003), p. 26. Wilken quotes Evagrius in introducing his own attempt to see the church fathers in a different way. He goes on to say: "On page after page the reader senses that what they [the early Christian thinkers] believe is anchored in regular, indeed habitual, participation in the church's worship, and what they teach is confirmed by how they pray," pp. 26–27.

4 Irenaeus, *Against Heresies,* book 4, chapter 18, section 5.

5 Gregory of Nyssa, *Against Eunomius*, book III.

6 Evelyn Underhill to A.B. Quinquagesima [Sunday before Ash Wednesday], 1936, in *The Letters of Evelyn Underhill*, ed. Charles Williams (London and New York: Longmans, Green and Co., 1943), p. 252.

7 Evelyn Underhill to L.K., Lammas Day [1 August], 1937, in *The Letters of Evelyn Underhill*, p. 259.

8 Evelyn Underhill to A.M.J., 13 December 1934, in *The Letters of Evelyn Underhill*, p. 240

9 Evelyn Underhill, *Practical Mysticism* (1914) (Mineola, NY: Dover Publications, 2000), p. 84.

10 Alain de Botton, *Status Anxiety* (London: Penguin, 2004), p. 238.

11 The pagan critic Caecilius, in Minucius Felix, *Octavius*, 8.4 (Carthage c. 200).

12 Patricia J. Williams, *Seeing a Colour-Blind Future: The Paradox of Race* (London: Virago, 1997), p. 4. See also her *The Alchemy of Race and Rights: Diary of a Law Professor* (Cambridge, MA: Harvard University Press, 1992), and *The Rooster's Egg: On the Persistence of Prejudice* (Cambridge, MA: Harvard University Press, 1997). I provide a brief introduction to her work in *Divided Cities*, ed. Richard Scholar (Oxford: Oxford University Press, 2006), pp. 52–55.

13 W. Morrison (trans.), *Calvin's Commentaries: A Harmony of the Gospels of Matthew, Mark and Luke, Volume I* (Edinburgh: Saint Andrew Press, 1972), p. 295

14 C. F. Evans, *Saint Luke* (London: SCM Press, 1990), p. 396

15 See the obituary of Shirley Chisholm in *The New York Times*, January 3, 2005. http://www.nytimes.com/2005/01/03/obituaries/03chisholm.html?adxnnl=1&pagewanted=2&adxnnlx=1312235138-aGZRyFHJVxN72Zz8gKKK6g

16 http://www.dailymail.co.uk/news/article-1375952/We-forgive-easily-says-Archbishop-Canterbury.html#ixzz1TpK5GPax

17 http://theforgivenessproject.com/

18 James Alison, *Faith Beyond Resentment: Fragments Catholic and Gay* (London: Darton, Longman and Todd, 2001), p. 27. This is the opening of a chapter called "Theology amidst the Stones and Dust."

19 Molly Peacock, "Forgiveness" in *Cornucopia: New and Selected Poems 1975–2002* (New York: W.W. Norton & Co., 2002), p. 227. Copyright © 1995 by Molly Peacock. Used by permission of W. W. Norton & Company, Inc.

20 *The Selected Poetry of Yehuda Amichai,* edited and translated by Chana Bloch and Stephen Mitchell (Berkeley, Los Angeles and London: University of California Press, 1996), p. 34. Reproduced with permission of University of California Press.

21 Donna Tartt, *The Little Friend* (London: Bloomsbury, 2002).

22 *Confronted by God: The Essential Verna Dozier.* Eds. Cynthia Shattuck and Fredrica Harris Thompsett (New York: Seabury Books, 2006), p. 49.

23 Henry Chadwick, *East and West: The Making of a Rift in the Church* (Oxford: Oxford University Press, 2003), p. 1.

24 Chadwick, *East and West.* On beards see p. 12; on bread pp. 236, 239–243; on differences in theology see chapters 4 and 6 and passim.

25 For an introduction to the thought of Denys, see Andrew Louth, *Denys the Areopagite* (New York and London: Continuum, 1989).

26 See R. H. Lightfoot, *Locality and Doctrine in the Gospels* (London: Hodder and Stoughton, 1938) and *The Gospel Message of St Mark* (Oxford: Clarendon Press, 1950).

27 Evelyn Underhill to D.E. 25 October (undated, probably 1934) in *The Letters of Evelyn Underhill*, p. 224.

28 Dozier, *Confronted by God*, p. 156.

29 Virginia Hamilton Adair, *Beliefs and Blasphemies: A Collection of Poems* (New York: Random House, 1998), pp. 80–81. Copyright © 1998 by Virginia Hamilton Adair. Used by permission of Random House, Inc.

30 For more discussion of this, see Christopher Rowland, *Blake and the Bible* (New Haven and London: Yale University Press, 2010), especially pp. 224–225.

31 Ed. Deborah Hart, *Grace Cossington Smith* (Canberra: National Gallery of Australia, 2005), p. 74.

32 William James, *Varieties of Religious Experience* (1902).

33 W. R. Inge, *Personal Religion and the Life of Devotion* (London: Longmans, Green and Co., 1924), p. 38.

34 Deborah Hart, *John Olsen* (Sydney: Fine Art Publishing, 2002 [1st edition 1991]), p. 102.

35 Evelyn Underhill to M.R., 30 December 1907, in *The Letters of Evelyn Underhill*, p. 70.

36 Drusilla Modjeska, *Stravinsky's Lunch* (Sydney: Picador, 1999), p. 322.

37 Evelyn Underhill, *Worship* (London: Nisbet & Co, 1936), p. 3.

38 Evelyn Underhill to Marjorie Robinson, 6 February 1912, in *The Making of a Mystic. New and selected Letters of Evelyn Underhill,* ed. Carol Poston (Urbana, IL: University of Illinois Press, 2011), pp. 192–193. The Tyrrell she refers to was George Tyrrell, an Irish Jesuit priest, who was excommunicated for his modernist ideas. He died in 1909, three years before she wrote this letter.

39 Underhill, *Mysticism*, p. 296.

40 David Stancliffe, *God's Pattern: Shaping our Worship, Ministry and Life* (London: SPCK, 2003), p. 32.

41 Underhill, *Worship*, p. 98.

42 Stancliffe, *God's Pattern*, p. 2.

43 Paul S. Fiddes, *Participating in God. A Pastoral Doctrine of the Trinity* (London: Darton, Longman and Todd, 2000).

44 Inge, *Personal Religion and the Life of Devotion*, p. 39.

45 *Common Worship* (London: Church House Publishing, 2000), p. 182.

46 *Epistle to Diognetus*, Chapter V (late second century).

47 I have borrowed this term from my friend Vincent Strudwick, who has commented in a number of lectures and written in various unpublished writings on the distinction between the church gathered and the church dispersed.

48 Dozier, *Confronted by God*, pp. 147–148.

49 See Grace Davie, "Vicarious Religion: A Methodological Challenge" in Nancy Ammerman, ed. *Everyday Religion:*

*Observing Modern Religious Lives* (Oxford, England: Oxford University Press, 2007), pp. 21–35.

50 See Diana Eck, *A New Religious America: How a "Christian Country" Has Now Become the World's Most Religiously Diverse Nation* (San Francisco: Harper San Francisco, 2001).

51 Catherine Fox, *Love for the Lost* (London: Penguin, 2000), pp. 390–391.

52 Sara Miles, *Take This Bread: A Radial Conversion* (New York: Ballantine Books, 2007), p. xiii. See also Sara Miles, *Jesus Freak: Feeding, Healing, Raising the Dead* (San Francisco: Jossey-Bass, 2010).

53 Stancliffe, *God's Pattern*, p. 34.

54 Sigmund Freud, "The Uncanny" (1919) (London: Penguin, 2003).

55 In *American Primitive*, Mary Oliver (New York: Back Bay Books, 1983).